This Is When We Begin to Fight gives eloquent testimony to the twofold apostolate of life, rooted in love of God and, therefore, in love of the family and homeland. I highly recommend Steve Karlen's testimony and trust that it will inspire many to become soldiers of life, even as it encourages the many who are already engaged in the daily battle which brings the victory of life.

— **Raymond Leo Cardinal Burke**, Prefect Emeritus
of the Supreme Tribunal of the Apostolic Signatura

As a father who lost a child to abortion, I am inspired by Steve's candid call-to-action for all pro-life individuals, especially men, to fight the most important evil of our time. *This Is When We Begin to Fight* renews my hope that our generation will see the end of abortion in our nation, and it will compel you to fight for life as you witness what can happen when even just one individual works to enact change in his or her community.

— **Jason Jones**, President and Founder of Movie
to Movement, Producer, Author, Activist, and
Human Rights Worker

A moving narrative of one man whose experience . . . shows us that anyone and everyone can do something transformative for the Lord . . . a narrative of hope and courage, rooted in an inexorable trust in Almighty God.

— **The Most Rev. Donald J. Hying**, Bishop of Madison

We often hear that men shouldn't have a voice in the pro-life debate. This story of an average sports-loving guy proves that one man's voice can make a huge difference in the fight for the unborn. It's an inspiring read for men and women alike."

— **Carrie Gress**, Author of *The Anti-Mary Exposed*
and *Theology of Home*

Touching, honest, compelling. I wanted to cheer each spiritual transformation as the grip of the world gave way to the embrace of Our Lord. Steve Karlen's writing is engaging, passionate, stirring, funny, and down-to-earth. I couldn't put this book down.

— **Fr. Rick Heilman,** Founder of the Knights
of Divine Mercy

This book has truly blessed me in my own journey in the pro-life movement as a former abortion worker. Steve helped me realize that no matter what we face in this journey, we are not alone. God is always with us.

— **Myra Neyer,** Former Abortion Worker

[It is] the spiritual journey of one of those good men who could not sit idle on the roadside of life and allow the evil of abortion to triumph. This book bears witness to the passionate commitment of Steve Karlen and many others to defending every precious gift of life from its first moment of conception.

— **The Most Rev. Thomas J. Olmsted,** Bishop of Phoenix

Giving voice not only to the voiceless pre-born but to so many who work tirelessly yet silently in advocacy on their behalf, Steve captures the spiritual highs and despairing lows that come with this particular mission and reminds us that each new day is another time when we renew our commitment to life—a new day when we begin to fight.

— **Monica Doumit,** Director of Public Affairs and
Engagement, Catholic Archdiocese of Sydney

The City of Oakland put me in jail for carrying a sign that said "God Loves You And Your Baby. Let Us Help You" outside an abortion clinic. In jail, I ministered to broken men, many of whom had realized sitting on the "sideline" of the abortion controversy cost them the lives of their sons and daughters. Had I been able to put Steve's book in their hands when my time in jail ended, I would have been able to continue to reach, heal, and inspire their hearts.

— **Rev. Walter Hoye II**, Founder and President,
Issues4Life Foundation

THIS IS WHEN

WE BEGIN

TO

FIGHT

**A family's battle against late-term abortion,
academia . . . and miscarriage at home.**

STEVE KARLEN

Cappella
Books
Nashville, Tennessee

For information, write to Cappella Books, P.O. Box 50358, Nashville, TN 37205.

Cover design: Jeanette Gillespie
Interior layout and e-book: LParnell Book Services

ISBN: 978-1-7327417-6-8 (Print)

Printed in the United States of America

27 26 25 24 23 22 21 20   1 2 3 4 5

For Laura,
my beloved, a hero of this story and the hero of our family.

For Peter, John Paul, Teresa,
Katherine, and Benedict,
who daily remind me what a treasure the gift of life is.

And for Gianna and Gerard,
*who inspire me to strive for heaven
that I may one day finally meet you.*

Contents

∿∿ ∿∿ ∿∿

The light shines in the darkness,
and the darkness has not overcome it.
— JOHN 1:5

All things work for good for those who love God.
— ROMANS 8:28

The Mighty One has done great things
for me, and holy is his name.
— LUKE 1:49

Foreword

~~~

This is more than just a book. This is a journey.

On one level, it's a journey of a pro-life leader and his family, who are led by God's grace and His people, by personal tragedy and community challenges, through the joys and sorrows of fighting abortion.

On another level, it's a journey that many of us have made and many more are called to make, as our world continues to be immersed in the greatest human rights struggle of all time, which is abortion.

The journey is intensely personal and yet involves the most basic instincts and principles that unite all humanity. It's about rediscovering the value of a human life and harnessing the most basic human response to the killing of children.

As I travel the nation equipping pro-life activists, I point out that the starting point of our efforts to end abortion *is a broken heart*. "Blessed are they who mourn, for they will be comforted" (Matthew 5:4). We need to look the unborn child in the eye and come face to face with the violence that abortion does to that child. We have to *let it break our hearts*. Then, with tears in our eyes, and our hearts broken wide open, God will be able to fill those hearts with the grace we need to *do something* about this violence.

The abortion "issue" has become too abstract. Amidst the philosophical, moral, religious, and constitutional arguments—all of which have their place—we can sometimes end up thinking that abortion is ultimately a *debate* or a difference of opinions, albeit strong opinions.

But abortion is not so much about beliefs as about *bloodshed*; not so much about viewpoints as about *victims*. Some who support abortion say we should "agree to disagree." But when violence is being carried out, we don't sit back and *agree to disagree* with the perpetrator. *Rather, we stop the perpetrator.*

And that's the line we have to learn to cross regarding abortion. Some say that while they would never have an abortion, it's "none of their business" to stop someone else from getting one. This view, of course, forgets about the victim who needs our defense. We don't hear people speaking this way, for instance, about child abuse. "I don't believe in abusing my child, but if someone else wants to abuse theirs, it's none of my business; let them have their choice."

This book shows us how we cross that line from the abstract abortion debate to the concrete saving of its victims. The journey outlined in this book is about how we connect with the *humanity of these children* and, in so doing, allow that most basic human response of *protecting our children* to impel us into the effort to end abortion.

Steve Karlen and his family have made this journey, and this book expresses so well how the mind, the emotions, the relationships, the hopes, the fears, the energy, and the exhaustion of engaging the abortion battle can lead a person to be ***all in*** on behalf of the weakest and most vulnerable children, the unborn.

So many passages in this book capture, in one instant, that human connection that's so necessary to ending abortion. One of my favorite passages is when Steve relates how a passerby stopped to read a brochure Steve was handing him about the violence of abortion. The man was stunned and simply asked, "Is this real?" and when Steve said it was, the man left, devastated.

There it is. That is what happened to Steve and his family; that is what happened to that man, who was open to the truth. And that is what pro-life activism strives to accomplish—and is accomplishing—across America and around the world.

It begins with the most obvious evil: *late-term abortion.* Every abortion is wrong, without exception. But it is much easier to awaken the conscience of America by exposing late-term abortion than early abortion. We always move people from the more obvious to the less obvious.

And to move them away from abortion means to move them into the streets, as 40 Days for Life—an effort I've been blessed to be part of from its inception and that Steve is privileged to help lead—is doing so well.

The pro-life movement is not called together from above; it arises from the hearts and souls and kitchen tables and families of America, who know they cannot stand idly by while children are being killed. This is why the pro-life movement is so large, so diverse, and simply doesn't go away. It can't. It is a movement as resilient as humanity itself.

And the battle this movement calls us to is not something we fit into our comfortable lives. *On the contrary, we have to fit our lives into the battle.*

I often relate the story of the public official who once took his young daughter through the Holocaust Memorial in Washington, D.C. She was saying nothing but holding his hand tighter and tighter as they went past the various disturbing displays. At the end was a guest book; the dad looked over his daughter's shoulder as she signed it. He knew he had done the right thing by bringing her because she then wrote in the book, *"Why didn't somebody DO something?"*

This book, this journey, will bless you. Take its challenge. Let your heart be broken. And follow Steve's example of saying yes to the wondrous grace that never lets us off the hook but never lets us down.

Fr. Frank Pavone, National Director, Priests for Life
President, National Pro-life Religious Council

Introduction

∿

Half of the population is pro-life, but far fewer choose to do something about it. Men, in particular, tend to sit on the sidelines of the abortion controversy. It's long been an issue that we've been told we aren't entitled to form an opinion on.

"My body, my choice."

"You can't get pregnant."

"No uterus, no opinion."

"Another white man telling women what to do with their bodies."

For most of us, we just think, *Why risk being ostracized as a "misogynist" for standing up for life when it's far more comfortable to pour a beer, grab a slice of pizza, and sit down to watch the game?*

But, for better or for worse, we live at a time when that's simply not an option. Men can no longer stand on the sidelines and hope for the best for our lives, our families, and our communities. Not when abortion is the leading cause of death not only in our country but also in our world. Not when a million little boys and girls lose their lives to abortion each year in the most prosperous country in the history of civilization. Not when abortion ends more lives worldwide than all other causes of death *combined.*

A simple look at the numbers proves that abortion isn't just a political issue. It's not only a "social issue" (whatever that means). It's the greatest human rights crisis the world has ever seen.

But ultimately, the women getting abortions are neither numbers nor statistics. They're our friends. They're our family members. Our co-workers, neighbors, classmates—even the people we go to church with are having abortions. And every abortion leaves in its wake a devastating trail of heartache and destruction. There is, of course, the baby, whose life is lost. There's also a mother scarred. A father wounded. Four grandparents who will never hold their grandchild. Aunts, uncles, nieces, nephews, and surviving and future siblings. Our entire society has been hurt—directly or indirectly—by abortion, and it's these women, men, and children harmed by abortion who compel us to speak up.

Every active pro-lifer has his or her own reason for standing up in defense of human life. Some had the sanctity of life reinforced at home in a family that made praying in front of an abortion facility a routine part of life. Some had their eyes opened to the horror of abortion by a pro-life sermon at church later in life. Many have had personal experiences with abortion—or saw how abortion wreaked havoc on the life of a loved one. But the common thread all active pro-lifers share is that they took a leap of faith to stand up and serve the least of our brothers and sisters: unborn children and their mothers who are in danger of being victimized by a billion-dollar abortion industry.

We cannot continue to remain silent. We are seeing what happens because of this silence. Abortion shatters relationships, destroys families, and threatens even the very fabric of the communities we live and work in. Decades later, women *and* men continue to struggle with the trauma caused by a choice that was sold to them as a solution to their problems.

I never expected that agreeing to accompany my wife at my first-ever pro-life vigil was the first step of a journey that would lead to me one day speaking about abortion to fifty thousand people at a time—or rallying prayer warriors in Mexico or leading a fifty-state pro-life bus tour. That's not an attempt to "humblebrag" because the stories I've shared from coast to coast aren't of my own making. They're the work of God—I'm just blessed to have had a front-row seat. And if God can use a guy like me to spread the Gospel of Life, He absolutely can use you.

But He needs your "yes" first. And that's my prayer with this book—to show you that God can take even the most reluctant "yes" and use it to save a life, save a soul, and leave an indelible mark on the world that will have a generational impact.

And, trust me, you'll still find time for a beer, a slice of pizza, and the game.

We gave it our best shot, but when the University of Wisconsin Hospital and Clinics Authority Board members cast their votes, eleven members of the board voted to approve performing late-term abortions adjacent to the University of Wisconsin campus. Only three voted to oppose.

Filled with bitterness and more than a little self-pity, I relayed the news to one of my fellow pro-lifers—an old Army chaplain who had been fighting for abortion-vulnerable moms and babies since long before I was even born.

His sharp rebuke caught me by surprise.

"Of course, you lost! You haven't been at this pro-life work very long, have you? This is when we *begin* to fight!"

1

The Text Message

~~~

Walking into work that brisk January morning, the text message I received from my brand-new bride probably should have been my first clue that something was wrong. For reasons I still don't quite understand, Laura hates sending text messages. She doesn't even like to receive them. But as I walked into my downtown Chicago office that winter day back in 2007, something led her to make an exception.

Sure enough, there was trouble. Half an hour earlier, my wife was, herself, on the way to work when she received a phone call from her friend, Jessica, who announced she was pregnant.

"But don't worry," Jessica assured Laura. "I'm going to get an abortion."

To make matters worse, all of Jessica's other friends affirmed that decision to terminate her pregnancy.

"You've got to do what's right for you," they said. "You've got to look out for yourself. You've got to look out for *your* future. Don't let anybody try to tell you this is some kind of moral decision."

Laura woke up that morning considering herself to be "pro-choice." It wasn't so much that she was radically pro-abortion. But somewhere along the line, she had fully embraced moral relativism and the tired refrain of "I wouldn't choose to have an abortion, but it's not my place to judge someone who does." Her world was one where, perhaps, the greatest sin—maybe the only sin—one could commit was to offend someone. A bleeding-heart liberal, Laura leaned left on most issues.

But to learn that a friend was pregnant and planning to end the life of her child forced Laura to reexamine her pro-choice stance. It was one thing to condone abortion as a nebulous "social issue" that's discussed vaguely and only in the context of electoral politics. It became quite a different matter when understood in the context of a real mother, a real baby, and a real life at stake. With Jessica preparing to schedule an abortion, time was at a premium. Everyone in Jessica's life was urging her to end the pregnancy. If anybody was going to advocate for Jessica and for her baby, it was going to have to be us.

THREE STEPS TO SAVE A LIFE

While Laura had been ambivalent toward abortion, I was staunchly pro-life. But while I had always been pro-life, I never really did much about it. I don't know whether that's because I was lazy. Maybe it's because I didn't know what I could do—beyond voting pro-life—to really make a difference. But for one reason or another, I never acted on that conviction that every human life is sacred and precious and needs to be actively defended.

Still, I was vocal enough about my position on the issue that Laura knew to talk to me when Jessica announced her abortion plans that morning. After I received Laura's text, we spent the next hour trading messages to set our three-step strategy for reaching out to empower Jessica to keep her baby.

First, we offered to let Jessica move in with us and stay rent-free. This was especially important because she was in a difficult financial position, always struggling to make ends meet—and often behind on paying her rent. That's why the second part of our plan was to offer Jessica financial support. Laura and I had gotten married only six months earlier and were blessed with many generous gifts of money from family and friends. We couldn't allow financial considerations to pressure Jessica into having an abortion. The money was hers if she needed it. The third part of our plan was the boldest. Laura—just months away from giving birth herself—offered to adopt Jessica's baby if that's what it would take to give her the courage she needed to choose life. Imagine that! An hour ago, Laura considered herself pro-choice. Now she was offering to adopt a baby in danger of abortion. Perhaps we, still newlyweds, were about to become a family of *four*.

The days that followed were something of a roller coaster ride. Jessica was receptive to Laura's encouragement, but other obstacles emerged. For one, Jessica was battling a serious illness. That illness would not make the pregnancy dangerous for Jessica or her baby, but according to her doctors, her medications could *possibly* lead to a birth defect.

"What kind of birth defect?" I asked Laura.

"Gastroschisis—it's usually treatable and almost always survivable. It's basically a messed up abdominal wall that needs to be repaired after birth."

"There's going to be a lot more messed up than this baby's abdominal wall if she has an abortion!" I shouted.

Looking back, it's clear my bitter response was an indicator that I was missing the big picture. Throughout Laura's conversations with her friend, it was difficult for me to understand Jessica's decision-making process, particularly the apparent flippancy with which she suggested she wasn't interested in making an adoption plan. "I'm not worried about parenting," she said. "I just don't want to be pregnant for nine months."

But what I foolishly dismissed as flippancy should have been a warning sign—a big, bright, neon, flashing warning sign—desperately trying to tell us, *You're not meeting her needs!* To me, it seemed so simple. If Jessica needed shelter, money, or an adoptive family, we'd give it to her, save the day, and everybody would live happily ever after. I completely failed to grasp the complex and intricate tapestry of fears, anxieties, and pressures that leads a woman to contemplate abortion. In reality, it was *I* who was being flippant.

Laura continued to talk with Jessica and to bring calm to the situation. We breathed a sigh of relief when we learned that Jessica would be breaking the news that she was expecting to her family. One usually doesn't share news of a pregnancy with loved ones only to have an abortion. Plus, Jessica came from a Christian family, so maybe her relatives would be able to comfort her and counter the influence of those in her life urging her to terminate.

We were sorely disappointed when many of Jessica's loved ones joined the chorus of voices suggesting she end her child's life, but it was still far too early to give up. Laura began sharing fetal development information with Jessica. Laura always loved reading pregnancy websites to track the progress of our own pregnancy. Every Sunday morning as she entered a new week of gestation, she eagerly shared with me a series of milestones describing just how her pregnancy was unfolding. We found it especially fun to use these websites to track our tiny baby's growth.

"Ooh! Our baby is the size of a pomegranate!"

"Ummm . . . how big is a pomegranate?"

"About five inches."

"OK!"

The week-by-week roadmap through pregnancy really served to humanize our unborn child—especially during that first trimester. We thought it would be important for Jessica to have the same experience, particularly when it was still far too early for her to feel the baby kick. Perhaps reading about her baby's taste buds and developing fingers and toes would touch Jessica's heart and help her fall in love with her baby. But while I thought it was important for Jessica to learn about fetal development, I failed to ask myself, "What does *Jessica* think is important?" I certainly didn't mean to fulfill the pro-abortion stereotype that pro-lifers are obsessed with babies but couldn't care less about mothers. We sincerely wanted to do everything we could to assist and empower Jessica. But my tunnel-vision focus on saving a baby from abortion kept me from putting myself in her shoes and figuring out how we could best give her the support she needed.

Ultimately, Laura's encouragement did seem to make a difference. Jessica decided to keep her baby, and in a matter of days, she went from planning to have an abortion to picking out names. If it turned out the baby was a girl, Jessica would name her daughter Gabriela.

Laura and I were so happy. We were so excited for a tragedy averted. We were so delighted that we could play some small role in this life saved. Above all, we were thrilled for Jessica, for her baby, and for this new journey they'd begin *together*.

Or so we thought.

THE PHONE CALL

A few days later, some of Laura and Jessica's mutual friends organized a dinner with Jessica. After everybody got off work one afternoon, we met at a restaurant downtown.

I was eager to meet Jessica, but she never showed up.

Her phone was turned off, so we left a couple of messages. Jessica's absence wasn't a huge surprise. She was still in her first trimester, so maybe she was feeling ill. Or perhaps there was confusion over the date, time, or location. Whatever kept Jessica from joining us at dinner, we'd find out soon enough.

Indeed, we did.

On Sunday morning, we woke up, went to church, came home, and had lunch. Right as we were starting to clear the table and wash the dishes, Laura's phone rang.

She answered it.

It was Jessica.

Jessica was sobbing.

I only heard one half of the conversation. But when I heard Laura tell Jessica, "I believe you. I know you didn't mean to hurt anybody," I put together the pieces. While we were at the restaurant just a few nights earlier, she was having an abortion. She had been able to withstand the pressure from her friends and even from her own family members. But, when she was pressured by her doctor, it broke her. She gave in. She had the abortion. And now here she was on the phone, heartbroken, devastated, never to be the same. Laura later told me doctors suggested abortion because Jessica faced a high risk of miscarrying.

As Laura tried to console Jessica, I ran out of the room, racked with grief. I was dizzy. I wanted to kick something. More constructively, I promised myself that from that moment on, whatever I could do to prevent even one more baby like Jessica's from being lost to abortion, I would do it.

I also promised myself I'd do whatever I could to prevent even one more heart like Jessica's from being broken by abortion. Because not only was Jessica's baby violated; Jessica was too. How could her doctor push her to have an abortion? She was already struggling with an illness. Didn't the doctor know that women who have had abortions are significantly more likely to commit suicide?[1] Didn't the doctor know that abortion significantly increases the risk of depression, hospitalization for psychiatric care, substance abuse, anxiety, and a host of other mental health problems?[2] The last thing she needed was an abortion.

Right after Jessica recovered from the physical trauma of her abortion, she suddenly moved to another state, and we lost touch with her. In fact, Jessica's Sunday afternoon telephone call to share the news of her abortion was the last conversation she and Laura ever had. Jessica wasn't bitter toward us, and Laura certainly had no intention of turning her back on her kindhearted friend. But the painful juxtaposition of Laura giving birth shortly after Jessica had her abortion proved to be too much for Jessica to continue their friendship.

The loss of both Jessica's baby and Laura's friendship with her brought me to a moment of reckoning. We naively thought we saved Jessica and her baby from abortion, but we didn't. The realization that this was no "happily ever after" fairy tale forced me to ask and answer some hard questions: What could I have done differently? What should I have done differently?

Years later, I ask myself the same questions. What if I hadn't made so many assumptions about what Jessica needed? What if, instead of popping champagne corks after Jessica told us she was choosing life, I got online and found a pregnancy center to assist her in seeing that decision through? What if I had listened more and spoken less? What if I had seen Jessica's plan to have an abortion as a cry to be heard rather than as a problem to be solved? Maybe, just maybe, with a little more wisdom and maturity on my part, Jessica's story would have had a happy ending.

Of course, it's much too early to talk about the ending of Jessica's story. Her story is far from over because our God is one of redemption—a God who loves to bring good out of evil. A God who promises us that "all things work for good for those who love God" (Romans 8:28). There's great reason to hope that Jessica will one day soon join the countless post-abortive women now praying in front of the facility where she had her abortion, leading a post-abortion healing retreat, or volunteering in her pregnancy center—if she hasn't done so already. So we pray and we trust in the Lord, who tells us, "Behold, I make all things new" (Revelation 21:5).

My story wasn't over either. Only after years of prayer would I realize how God used my failure to save Jessica and her baby from abortion to bring good out of evil in my life, to increase my faith, to draw me closer to my wife, and even to help save the lives of other abortion-vulnerable children.

2

Liberal Activist and Teenage Republican Get Married and Have a Baby

～～

You don't see a lot of love stories about a guy who spent his teenage years volunteering as a Republican operative going on to marry a liberal Democrat who marched with the International Socialist Organization.

Actually, political differences might not even have been the greatest source of surprise when it came to our relationship. I'm a lifelong Green Bay Packer backer while Laura's Windy City roots mean she grew up a fan of the dreaded Chicago Bears. (Perhaps it's true that opposites attract!) It's also possible that our unexpected pairing boils down to processed meat. Between Chi-Town Italian sausage and Wisconsin bratwurst, we found common ground in grilled, tube-shaped sausages.

When we got engaged, Laura discussed waiting five years after marriage to have kids. We needed time to travel, to build wealth, to have fun, and to do all those other super-ficial things that cause people to put off having children.

I thought five years might be a little excessive. I had looked forward to getting married and having children since I was a child myself, but I didn't force the issue. Quite frankly, I was just happy this beautiful, intelligent, and talented woman was willing to spend the rest of her life with me.

Eventually she softened her waiting period to two years. Only weeks before we married, however, she received a pre-liminary diagnosis of polycystic ovarian syndrome, and doc-tors told her we shouldn't expect to have any children. At the time, I was grappling with the Catholic teaching prohibiting the use of contraception and selfishly thought perhaps my bride-to-be's infertility might be a blessing in disguise.

Nevertheless, only two months after our wedding day, Laura said she thought she might be pregnant and bought a pregnancy test. We couldn't bear the thought of watching and waiting, wondering exactly when the answer would appear, so we set a timer for three minutes and left the room to say a prayer. I'll never forget the moment we walked back in and saw the test with a positive result. Not knowing what to say, the two of us just laughed with joy in our tiny, one-bedroom, Chicago apartment. When I had woken up that Sunday morning, fatherhood was the farthest thing from my mind, but suddenly *I was a dad*. We had entered into the greatest of mysteries: the creation of life. Three months earlier, I had been a college student, eating pizza three times a week and staying up all night playing the *Madden 2004* video game. Now I was a husband and a father of a child I'd have to name and provide for and protect.

For a woman who previously had little interest in having babies, Laura *loved* being an expectant mother. When we went out to purchase decor to celebrate our first Christmas together, her eye caught sight of an adorable ornament depicting a mommy, daddy, and baby penguin playing in the snow. She spun around and looked at me with a smile so radiant my heart still melts each December when I put it on the tree.

By the time Jessica had her abortion, my wife had nearly seven months of these moments—nearly seven months' worth of experience knowing what it means to carry the gift of human life. That firsthand experience with the joys of motherhood made the Jessica ordeal all the more devastating for Laura.

CRACKS IN THE FACADE

After graduation, Laura had spurned a prestigious job offer that involved planning events to honor wealthy donors at Northwestern University. Ever the bleeding heart, she instead pursued a job as a bilingual social worker serving people with mental illness on Chicago's South Side. Though she wasn't trained in social work, being fluent in Spanish qualified her for at least an interview.

After the on-the-job interview, Laura wasn't sure her Spanish was quite strong enough to land the position. Even after a language immersion program that took her to Ecuador for a semester, her education still hadn't exactly covered how to discuss procuring an *enema*. She was similarly unfamiliar with other words that she'd need to know in a health-related field. Despite this, she landed the position and began spending her days assisting people with mental illness in some of the poorest neighborhoods in Chicago. The experience was interesting to say the least. Laura constantly found herself in situations that made me less than comfortable. One Saturday afternoon, we went for a drive so she could show me the neighborhoods where she had clients.

"If you think you see a drug deal going down, there's definitely a drug deal going down," she explained. "If you're not sure, there's definitely a drug deal going down. If you don't think there's a drug deal going down, well, there still might be a drug deal going down."

Sure enough, during our tour through the South Side, we saw a man being shaken down, pinned to a van.

Sometimes Laura's clients became aggressive or angry. One of them had previously killed a person. Sometimes Laura was sent into dangerous neighborhoods with the advice, "Go early, and the drug dealers will still be sleeping. And don't worry; nobody will bother you. You're a tiny white female, so they'll assume you're a cop." That's not exactly the day-to-day I envisioned for my wife, especially now that she was carrying our child. But Laura and her colleagues sincerely cared for their clients, so they did the best they could to empower these men and women to thrive in spite of their mental illnesses and their poverty. That meant trying to equip their clients for success by offering advice like "Try to quit smoking," or "Don't be promiscuous."

The problem is that Laura found many in her field wouldn't quit smoking and wouldn't quit being promiscuous. Some of their lives were marked with the same wreckage as the men and women they were trying to help. One night we attended a condo-warming party for one of Laura's co-workers. A television news story aired, discussing funding cuts for social work in the state of Illinois. Those cuts would affect Laura and her colleagues' organizational budget. The disgust in the room was palpable. For those present, it was simply taken as gospel that additional funding would lead to solutions for those facing mental illness.

Laura remained silent, but privately she began to doubt. "No matter how much help we offer," she said, "counseling and medication aren't enough. The clients whose conditions improve are the ones who want to get better and who draw near to their faith and their family."

It was one of the first cracks I saw in Laura's confidence in a secular salvation that assumed the correct bureaucratic structures could meet the deepest needs of the human person. It was only a matter of time before the entire edifice crumbled.

THE POLITICAL ELEPHANT IN THE ROOM

Since the earliest days of our relationship, our stark political differences always served as something of an elephant in the room. Laura and I started dating after meeting during our freshman orientation at the University of Wisconsin-Madison. We had similar interests but dramatically different ideas about the role of government in society. (And different ideas about nose rings—but that's another story.)

I entered college with great enthusiasm for living in Wisconsin's capital city. Having spent much of my high school career heavily involved in Republican politics, I couldn't wait to get closer to the action. As a teenager, I found myself disgusted and discouraged by the moral climate in 1990s America. My religious formation growing up was weak, but I generally knew right from wrong. As a sophomore in high school, I found myself isolated as friend after friend traded the values with which we were raised for fast cars, promiscuity, and an anything-goes morality that I couldn't comprehend. I was further troubled by similar developments at the national level. When President Bill Clinton vetoed the 1995 Partial Birth Abortion Ban Act, I was stunned. It wasn't only the veto that horrified me; it was the public's indifference toward a procedure that dismembered children on their way through the birth canal.

The final straw came when the nation collectively yawned at President Clinton's impeachment trial for lying under oath about committing adultery in the Oval Office. Something had to be done. I was convinced that our nation needed a leader with character. A leader who would have the drive and conviction to defend the moral law. A leader who would support and sign into law powerful pro-life legislation. A leader who would appoint pro-life Supreme Court justices to end abortion.

So I volunteered for George W. Bush's presidential campaign. I spent my evenings and weekends stuffing envelopes, making calls, and delivering campaign literature. I skipped school to hit the campaign trail, meeting the future president multiple times—including once on the White House lawn after he had taken office. Of course, none of my wild dreams for the Bush presidency were fulfilled, but my convictions never waned.

Laura came to Madison with decidedly *different* ideas. She had never intended to go to the University of Wisconsin. In fact, as she toured prestigious schools across the country, she had never even *heard* of the University of Wisconsin. When Laura's mother urged her to make the 150-mile drive from the Chicago suburbs to Madison to tour the school, she reluctantly agreed.

Not long after stepping foot on campus, Laura's initial reticence disappeared entirely. She was particularly drawn in by the school's history of liberal activism. While Madison has long been known as a progressive city, its reputation was solidified during the Vietnam War when anti-war protests turned into riots. Activists even bombed a university building where military research was being conducted, killing one researcher and injuring three others. The bombing is, perhaps, the best example of why former Wisconsin Governor Lee Dreyfus once referred to the city as "30 square miles surrounded by reality."[1]

While Laura certainly didn't condone violence, Madison's liberalism and its penchant for rebelling against authority won her over quickly. By the end of her visit to campus, her heart was set on attending the University of Wisconsin. It didn't even matter that as an out-of-state student, she'd need to pay sky-high tuition. "I'll do whatever it takes. I'll take out whatever loans I need to," she begged her parents, demonstrating the same fiscal sensibilities as the city she so desperately wanted to call home.

Laura's wish was granted, and within eighteen months, she'd be protesting shoulder-to-shoulder with socialists on the same ground where protests had turned into riots thirty-five years earlier. It took us more than a decade after graduation to finish making payments on her student loans!

For most of our dating relationship, Laura and I managed to tolerate each other's political beliefs, but there were moments of friction. For example, Laura didn't exactly appreciate it when I asked whether she was a communist. (I maintain it was a legitimate question.)

On campus in the fall of 2004, Laura joined eighty thousand John Kerry supporters[2]—including Bruce Springsteen and the Foo Fighters—for the biggest rally of that year's presidential campaign. On her way to the event, she passed by pro-life protesters and wondered what in the world they could possibly be thinking. Though we don't know exactly who those protesters were, many years later, we suspect we've probably hosted at least a few of them for dinner at our home.

Meanwhile, as the election neared, I was disgusted to think that Laura's vote would cancel out mine. So, I recruited a college classmate to vote for President Bush's re-election. He was completely apolitical, but he seemed to relish the mischievous prospect of voting for Bush to make sure that his vote would cancel out Laura's while mine would stand. Laura spent the day after Bush's re-election sulking. "Maybe in 2008, I can work to elect Barack Obama if he runs for president." I still like to tease Laura by reminding her she cast her first ballot of our married life together for disgraced former Illinois governor Rod Blagojevich, who was only recently released from federal prison for corruption. Now, she'll laugh with me. She still doesn't find it very funny, however, when I tease her the two times each year that my Packers beat up on her Bears.

Jessica's abortion changed her forever. In a very different way, it changed Laura forever as it led her to reexamine her previous convictions and embrace the pro-life position. And I was about to find out that Jessica's abortion was going to change me forever as well. Like Laura, I had never really had a personal encounter with abortion until Jessica's heartbroken phone call. It shook me to the core. I began to understand that something had to change. Yes, I had always been pro-life, but now I could see it wasn't enough for me to *be* pro-life. I had to do something about it.

Standing in my bedroom with my head spinning, my heart pounding, and the sound of her sobs still ringing in my ears, I thought about how Jessica was not an isolated case. A million Jessicas a year have their hearts broken by abortion—just in the United States. I certainly didn't have any political influence, and I didn't have much money to contribute to the pro-life cause. But it was time to turn off the football game and find a way to put into action my convictions about the sanctity of human life.

3

40 Days for Life

∾

That spring, Laura gave birth to a baby boy. We briefly considered naming him Isaac because, like Abraham and Sarah in the book of Genesis, we didn't expect to be blessed with a child. But I had long admired St. Peter. He was one of the biggest boneheads in all of sacred Scripture. After all, he's the disciple who repeatedly failed to trust in the Lord. He doubted that he could walk on water. He insisted that Christ not lay down His life. He ordered Jesus not to wash his feet. He denied the Lord three times. Even after the Resurrection, he needed to be corrected by St. Paul. He screwed up again and again and again. And yet, in spite of all his faults and failings, the Lord chose to make Peter the premier apostle, the first pope, the rock upon which Christ's Church would be built. And the gates of hell shall not prevail against it. If there was hope for Peter, maybe just maybe there was hope for a guy like me.

After Peter's birth, Laura left her job to become a stay-at-home mom. We quickly learned that Chicago was no place to try to raise a family on one tiny income. (Furthermore, after growing up in "America's Dairyland," I found the cheese selection was abysmal on the other side of the "Cheddar Curtain.") When our lease expired in June, we moved to a condo in Naperville, a town about thirty miles west of Chicago. Laura's parents had purchased it as an investment property and graciously allowed us to live there on very generous terms while I looked for a job in a more affordable community.

That same month, the Pro-Life Action League in Chicago learned that the country's biggest abortion provider, Planned Parenthood, was preparing to open a 22,000-square-foot abortion center in Aurora, a community adjacent to Naperville.[1] The facility would become one of the first of Planned Parenthood's abortion megacenters— gigantic abortion facilities designed to end the lives of preborn children in greater numbers and with greater efficiency than anything the Western world has ever seen. Scheduled to open on September 18, 2007, this particular Planned Parenthood location would become the largest abortion facility in the United States.[2]

Chicago's western suburbs comprise some of the country's most conservative communities, so it was no surprise that Planned Parenthood wasn't exactly advertising the groundbreaking for its new clinic. It was, however, shocking to see the great lengths to which the abortion giant was going in order to obscure its intentions.

Rumors began to swirl in Aurora when a local contractor started to suspect he was helping to build an abortion facility. After consulting with his pastor, the contractor left the project. Shortly thereafter, Pro-Life Action League's executive director, Eric Scheidler, used the Freedom of Information Act to learn that Gemini Office Development, a Planned

Parenthood front group, filed papers falsely saying the building would be a multiuse medical facility.[3] The claim couldn't have been further from the truth. From the beginning, the facility was designed to house one tenant: a Planned Parenthood abortion center.

As the summer heated up, so too did the controversy over the massive Planned Parenthood under construction. Scheidler and his team made a splash in both the media and Aurora City Council meetings. Laura and I followed the situation on the television evening news as thousands of pro-life Christians went into the streets for prayer vigils and demonstrations.

Before long, Laura and I started seeing flyers at church for something called 40 Days for Life. We learned that it was a peaceful campaign aimed at ending abortion through a forty-day campaign of prayer and fasting, community outreach, and a constant peaceful vigil in front of abortion centers.

Constant vigil? As in around the clock? Twenty-four hours a day? Never taking a break? Indeed, the Pro-Life Action League recruited volunteers to staff a vigil in front of the would-be Planned Parenthood for every second of the forty-day vigil that summer.

In the midst of all the excitement, Laura and I visited my parents in Appleton, Wisconsin. We saw 40 Days for Life posters there, too! It turns out this was becoming a nationwide effort. Three years earlier, the Brazos Valley Coalition for Life hosted a 40 Days for Life campaign with around-the-clock vigil coverage in front of the Planned Parenthood abortion facility in Bryan/College Station, Texas. During those forty days, the abortion rate dropped 28 percent.[4] One-by-one, cities across the United States adopted the model by launching their own 40 Days for Life vigils in front of their local abortion centers.

By 2007, the phenomenon was spreading so quickly that Shawn Carney and David Bereit, cofounders of the original 40 Days for Life campaign in Texas, answered the call to launch a coordinated 40 Days for Life campaign in cities across the country. Eighty-nine cities in thirty-three states joined the campaign in late September.

With Aurora's Planned Parenthood scheduled to open by then, Scheidler and the Pro-Life Action League started early, launching their campaign on August 9.[5] And when the City of Aurora delayed the opening of Planned Parenthood to investigate its deceptive paperwork, the vigil continued— running for fifty-three straight days before breaking.

I watched the Aurora campaign unfold from a distance. With a newborn baby and a ninety-minute, one-way commute into the city, I wasn't able to join the vigil. All my free time was spent submitting résumés and conducting interviews so that we could move our young family somewhere more affordable. But although I couldn't participate, I realized how, during Aurora's 40 Days for Life campaign, a pro-life giant had been awakened—even delaying the opening of one of America's largest abortion facilities for nearly two weeks.

Shortly after Labor Day, our prayers were answered as I accepted a job back in Madison. We were coming home. I still desired to make good on the promise I made the day I learned of Jessica's abortion, but our entry to the pro-life world unfolded slowly. Laura signed us up for the pro-life committee at our new church. The leader, Alissa, was looking to step down and invited us to chair the committee. She then added, "If you really want to get involved, you need to talk to Amy Hying."

Amy, we learned, headed up Madison's 40 Days for Life campaign. "Oh, that's the vigil we heard about in Aurora!" I told Laura. Yes, we definitely wanted to meet Amy.

Madison's next 40 Days for Life campaign wouldn't take place until the fall of 2008. But Amy and her group had been holding monthly prayer vigils at the two Madison Planned Parenthood facilities since the end of the 2007 fall campaign.

EXCUSES, EXCUSES

It was a sunny Saturday morning in early April when I asked Laura how she'd like to spend her day. The question was rhetorical. Baseball season had begun, and I had no intention of doing anything other than watching my beloved Milwaukee Brewers begin their race for the pennant. The team collapsed near the end of the 2007 season, narrowly missing a playoff berth for what would have been its first postseason appearance since before I was born. To add insult to injury, Milwaukee lost the National League Central Division to the Chicago Cubs—the Brewers biggest rival. Still working in Chicago at the time, I suffered amidst the many thousands of Cub fans at the office, on the "L" train, and everywhere else. I loathed those Cubs!

But 2008 was a new year. The team brought back stars like Prince Fielder, Rickie Weeks, Ben Sheets, and 2007 Rookie of the Year Ryan Braun. The streak of not making the playoffs for a quarter century—the longest such streak in professional sports—was due to end. And I'd spend my Saturday on the couch, from the first pitch to the post-game show.

It turns out Laura had other ideas. She answered my rhetorical question: "I thought maybe we could go to the vigil today."

"The vigil?" I stammered. "What vigil?"

"The 40 Days for Life group is going to be praying at Planned Parenthood today."

My stomach dropped. I needed an excuse . . . and fast.

"You know, Laura, I think it would be irresponsible to take Peter out in that cold weather. Maybe we can go in a month or two when it warms up," I suggested.

Laura responded, "Actually, it's not that cold today. The weather is much warmer than it looks outside."

"Yeah, but that wind. That's not going to be good for the baby at all."

"Steve, it's not windy outside."

I looked out the back door. It was a beautiful day, and the leaves on the trees were as still as could be. For a moment, I considered conjuring up a third reason we shouldn't go pray. But ultimately, I decided to spare myself the indignity of another lame excuse. We went to the vigil and prayed at the Planned Parenthood building near campus. The facility was rather run-down, and the lawn was strewn with garbage. Madison in the springtime is gorgeous, but you couldn't tell from the sidewalk in front of Planned Parenthood.

Even though it was located just blocks away from the house where Laura lived as a college senior, I didn't previously know there was a Planned Parenthood center near campus. The location wasn't a big surprise. It was an area well known for prodigious partying. The block adjacent to Planned Parenthood had been the site of some of the community's most notable protests during the Vietnam War. Over the years, those protests turned into a block party where thousands, or even tens of thousands, of people partied all day. In fact, the "Mifflin Street Block Party" would be held in just a few weeks. House parties on Mifflin Street made big money and competed for attendees by hosting bands or other artists. Each year, hundreds of "Mifflin" attendees were arrested for a wide variety of offenses. Those who weren't taken into custody often posed with accommodating police officers pretending to place them under arrest. Somewhere in an old shoebox, I have a picture of police officers mock arresting me and my old friend Adam Morse during our time on Mifflin Street.

Mifflin Street intersected with Washington Avenue, where Laura lived in college. Though it led to the state capitol, the blocks just east of the statehouse were more than a little shady. I half-jokingly referred to the area as the "Marijuana District." When there was an arrest, a robbery, or a sexual assault near campus, well, this is the area where it probably took place. One house down the block from Laura's was known to be a crack house.

When Laura returned to her house for the night, she would call me from the car and stayed on the phone with me until her front door was safely locked behind her. We hoped that this would deter any would-be assailants. At the very least, I'd be able to call the police in the event of an emergency.

Yes, this enclave of poor decision making was the perfect location for a Planned Parenthood clinic.

Laura and I had a hard time finding the vigil site. Planned Parenthood melded into its surroundings. As we looked, we encountered a well-dressed man coming down the sidewalk. He looked stunningly out of place in the neighborhood, so we asked him if he was going to the pro-life vigil. In fact, he was, and we followed him to Planned Parenthood.

The Planned Parenthood facility where we held vigil wasn't actually an abortion center, but it did sell abortions. A steady stream of couples made their way through the front doors of the building that Saturday morning, most likely to purchase the "morning after pill" to try to erase the consequences of bad decisions made on Friday night.

As shameful as my attempt to get out of joining the prayer vigil that morning was, my sloth disappeared quickly after we arrived. It was inspiring to see such a diverse crowd give up their Saturday morning to pray for an end to abortion. And for the first time, I saw something I'd come to observe again and again. I noticed that so many of the couples who entered the clinic rarely walked in side-by-side. I found it to be an interesting phenomenon. It wasn't uncommon for the boyfriends to heckle us as they passed by. Sometimes they'd raise their arms in triumph, as if to celebrate their conquest from the previous evening. Other times, a simple "[Expletive] you guys!" sufficed. But the bombastic bravado was a facade. For all their bluster, the boyfriends rarely had the courage to stand alongside their girlfriends. Instead, the girl might rush into the clinic, perhaps embarrassed by her boyfriend's juvenile behavior. Other times, she would linger behind, her eyes buried in the concrete sidewalk in shame. In either case, it was the eyes of the young women that fascinated me the most.

A popular cliché suggests "the eyes are the windows to the soul." For all of the abortion industry's rhetoric about reproductive freedom and empowering women, these women looked neither free nor empowered. Their hollow eyes revealed them to be broken shells of the women that God created them to be. Shells not unlike Jessica the day she called Laura in tears. My zeal was back.

As spring turned into summer, Laura and I continued to attend these Saturday morning pro-life vigils at Planned Parenthood. When Amy applied to lead the fall 40 Days for Life campaign, we were quick to volunteer for her leadership team. We had become so passionate about our pro-life mission that I couldn't wait to get through the workday so I could spend some time laboring to end abortion.

One Thursday afternoon, I went to confession at my parish. As I left, I noticed a van with a bumper sticker that read "Pro-Life Wisconsin." Eager to recruit more participants for 40 Days for Life, I got the attention of the vehicle's owner.

"Excuse me, sir . . ."

He turned toward me with an anxious look on his face. The man's children were playing in the mostly empty parking lot, and he thought I was about to inform him of some sort of mischief or behavior problem.

"No, no! It's not that. I just noticed your Pro-Life Wisconsin bumper sticker, and I wanted to ask whether you've ever heard of 40 Days for Life."

It turned out I was talking with Matt Sande, the director of legislation for Pro-Life Wisconsin. Of course, he knew all about 40 Days for Life! I felt a little bit silly, but we struck up a friendship quickly. In the months ahead, Matt became a mentor to me, helping to shape my understanding of the role of politics in abortion, the importance of praying in front of abortion facilities, and the necessity of pro-life men witnessing to the world through their love for their own families.

A Picture's Worth a Thousand Words

Madison's fall 2008 40 Days for Life campaign launched on Saturday, September 13 with a kickoff rally held in a local park. We opened the event with praise and worship music from a local musician, followed by a performance from a national Christian recording artist. Our guest speaker was photographer Michael Clancy, who shared the compelling story of the trials of growing up in an abusive family and his conversion to Christianity as an adult.[6]

Even more compelling, however, was the series of events that took place just months after he became a Christian, shaking the pro-life and secular worlds alike. In 1999, Michael was hired by *USA Today* to photograph a cutting-edge surgery performed on a twenty-one-week-old unborn baby named Samuel. Samuel had spina bifida, and doctors at Vanderbilt University were attempting a corrective procedure that risked inducing a premature delivery. If that were to happen, Samuel would not survive. The stakes were high, Michael said, and the operating room was filled with anxiety. Fortunately, the surgery was a success. As the tension dissipated, Michael describes what occurred next:

> A doctor asked me what speed of film I was using, out of the corner of my eye I saw the uterus shake, but no one's hands were near it. It was shaking from within. Suddenly, an entire arm thrust out of the opening, then pulled back until just a little hand was showing. The doctor reached over and lifted the hand, which reacted and squeezed the doctor's finger. As if testing for strength, the doctor shook the tiny fist. Samuel held firm. I took the picture! Wow! It happened so fast . . .[7]

It was another moment of conversion for Michael, who had long considered himself to be "pro-choice." The image of Samuel's tiny hand reaching out from the womb made it clear that the child in the womb is indeed a person. Still, these were the days before digital cameras became prevalent, so Michael had to submit his film to *USA Today* and then wait a week and a half to see whether the photograph actually turned out.

The picture was worth the wait. Ten days later, *USA Today's* photo editor called Michael, describing the photo as "the most incredible picture I've ever seen." Respected journalists suggested that the picture would be the frontrunner for that year's Pulitzer Prize.[8] Instead of receiving accolades, however, Michael found himself in the midst of a controversy.

In an article published by Gannett News Service, Dr. Joseph Bruner, who performed the surgery, described the photo as an "urban legend." He claimed it had been posed—that Samuel had not reached out on his own, but that Dr. Bruner pulled Samuel's arm out of the surgical opening himself. "The baby did not reach out," Bruner claimed. "The baby was anesthetized. The baby was not aware of what was going on."[9]

As I listened to Michael speak, I remember wondering whether it really made a difference how the photograph came to be. Whether Samuel reached for Dr. Bruner's finger or whether Dr. Bruner pulled Samuel's hand, the picture clearly illustrated a human hand and the undeniable humanity of a pre-born child. Even Dr. Bruner described Samuel as a "baby."

Nevertheless, Michael remained steadfast in his account of what transpired in the operating room, and he paid a price for it. Not only did Michael not win a Pulitzer Prize, but he said the controversy over the photograph also effectively ended his career as a photojournalist.

As Michael fought back tears, I became convinced of his sincerity. After years of favoring legal abortion, he had seen the truth about pre-born life. He refused to remain silent about the dignity of pre-born life even when speaking out meant the loss of his livelihood. In fact, Michael was so moved to share his story with as many people as possible that—even after traveling to Wisconsin from Tennessee—he didn't charge us an honorarium for speaking.

Michael Clancy's zeal made an impression on me. His visit to Madison was my first encounter with someone who made real and tremendous sacrifices to defend human life. It certainly wouldn't be the last.

4

A Few Good Men

~~~

For all the excitement I had for Madison's 40 Days for Life campaign to begin, I'm not quite sure I knew what I was getting myself into on day 1. But if I didn't know what I was getting myself into on day 1, the stakes of this spiritual battle became all too clear by the end of day 2.

Laura went out to pray in front of Planned Parenthood on the first day of the campaign. A young man approached her and shared the heartbreak he experienced when his girlfriend aborted their child. It happened again on day 2. Laura was out on the sidewalk when another man approached her and shared how he had recently gotten his girlfriend pregnant.

He wanted the baby. She wanted an abortion.

They argued about it.

She broke up with him.

She stole his credit card.

She used it to pay for her abortion.

And then, to pour salt on the open wound, she mailed him the sonogram image of his aborted baby.

I can't begin to imagine the degree of pain it must have taken to compel a complete stranger to share his story with my wife, but it was another sobering reminder that the devastating impact abortion has on mothers and fathers isn't just a talking point.

Amy, our campaign leader, knew this all-too-well. Her service in the pro-life movement gave her an eagle eye for women and men suffering in the aftermath of an abortion. During that first campaign, Laura and I marveled at Amy's ability to point out which angry passersby and hecklers were post-abortive. I found this gift of Amy's to be impressive. But more impressive was the compassion she had for post-abortive men and women.

It's no secret that our culture's discourse on abortion is polarizing. The temptation to demonize people on the other side of the issue is tremendous. All too often, rhetoric replaces dialogue. I certainly fell prey to that temptation. At the time, I was certain that Planned Parenthood's supporters and clients were evil people who needed to be defeated. But Amy didn't see them that way at all. She saw them as victims of a great lie, and she approached them with kindness.

Following our campaign midpoint rally that year, Laura and I joined Amy at a local fast-food restaurant for a meal. After ordering, Amy handed the cashier fliers on the Rachel's Vineyard post-abortion healing ministry. "I just wanted to give these to you because there are a lot of people hurting from abortion," she said. "And, if you know of anybody who is and who needs healing, please share this information."

I was stunned. *What is she doing? You can't just walk into a burger joint and start talking about abortion to the cashier! These people must think we are nuts!* I wanted to sink into the floor and escape this embarrassing display.

Amy couldn't have cared less of what the people in the restaurant thought of her. If somebody there that night needed the love of Christ, it was her calling to share it. It was an approach she modeled in every facet of her life. When she got married a little more than a year later, she and her husband Tom brought a bus of wedding attendees to Planned Parenthood to pray—on one of the coldest days of the year. Later, they held their reception in an old theater on an iconic pedestrian-traffic-only street frequented by students, tourists, and panhandlers. After dinner, some of the guests noticed that Amy and Tom were missing. Upon their return, they said they had stepped outside to greet some friends. The excuse was *technically* true, but I knew there was more to the story. I had left our wedding card for the happy couple in the car and went out to retrieve it. On my way to the parking garage, I saw Amy and Tom out in the frigid late-December Wisconsin night bringing food to the homeless who'd be sleeping on the streets that evening.

By the second week of the campaign, I was unemployed. We had moved back to Madison from Chicago when I accepted a position as a technical writer with a local software company. I assumed that my experience in journalism and my writing skills would make me a good fit for the job. But without a background in the inner workings of software, I struggled to tread water. My assumption that my writing ability qualified me to do technical writing was about as sound as assuming it qualified me to write music. I gave the job my best effort, but the handwriting was on the wall. My days were numbered.

Laura was able to find employment before I did, so she went back to work when I left the software company. It was not a joyful transition. During our engagement, Laura insisted she wanted to pursue a career even after having children. To give up a career to raise kids meant drudgery and subservience. But Peter's birth was a game-changer, as Laura fell in love with motherhood. It didn't take long for her to recognize there was deeper joy in taking care of her own flesh and blood than in being paid to help care for strangers as a social worker. She was not happy to go back to the workplace, but she did. And most importantly to me, she did it without complaining.

As a husband, I wasn't able to provide for my family. I was embarrassed and ashamed. But Laura never stopped encouraging me even as she, herself, was discouraged. We had reached the "for worse" and "in bad times" part of our vows, and she passed the test with flying colors.

While this change was painful, it did afford me the time to get more involved in 40 Days for Life. I quickly became one of the overnight shift regulars, praying in front of Planned Parenthood for an hour or two at a time in the middle of the night. Few sounds are more jarring and disorienting than an alarm going off at 2:30 in the morning prior to taking the 3:00-5:00 a.m. shift on the sidewalk in front of Planned Parenthood. (I learned it's a good idea to set a backup alarm after falling asleep again and getting a call asking where I was twenty-five minutes into my scheduled shift.)

The nights cooled off significantly as we marched toward November. I found that dressing in multiple layers is a necessity and I even picked out a pair of thick, heavy woolen socks, which remain my "campaign socks" for the cold nights on the sidewalk.

Trying to salvage every last minute of sleep, I calculated it took me about ten minutes to get bundled up to go. With next-to-no traffic on the streets in the wee hours of the morning, I could make it from my apartment on the West Side of Madison to Planned Parenthood on the East Side in just twenty minutes. If I managed to drive up to the vigil site before the dashboard clock read 3:01, I considered myself on time.

As difficult as it was to crawl out of bed and head over to those middle-of-the-night vigils, it was even more difficult to leave. Night after night, I found myself paired up with faithful men whose witness deeply inspired me. These were men of sacrifice whose love for the Lord, for pre-born children, and for abortion-vulnerable mothers was nothing short of heroic.

It's difficult to schedule an around-the-clock prayer vigil, and without the sacrifices of these men, it would have been impossible. Desperation was a regular part of filling the vigil schedule. As our role in Madison's campaign grew, Laura and I spent more and more time on the phone trying to fill the gaps.

"Hi Del, this is Laura Karlen from 40 Days for Life. We have a gap in our schedule from midnight to six o'clock on Tuesday morning. Do you think you could help us by taking some hours?"

"Sure! I'll take them."

"Great! Which ones?"

"All of 'em."

Del Teeter wasn't alone. Another core team member named Curt regularly worked second shift before spending the entire night—11:00 p.m. to 7:00 a.m.—out at the vigil. *What kind of man makes a commitment like that? Who are these guys?*

Over and over again, I found my prayer partners for the graveyard shift at Planned Parenthood were members of the Knights of Columbus. Inspired by their faithfulness, it wasn't long before I joined the Knights myself. I developed close friendships with the men I met out on the sidewalk. It turns out that when you meet someone willing to wake up in the middle of the night and go pray in front of an abortion center, you already have enough common ground that you can skip a few steps in the friend-making process.

While I made new friends, I was also delighted to be joined by an old friend on the sidewalk. Scrambling to schedule vigil hours, I went through my phone, my email address book, and my Facebook friend list to find people I could recruit. One of the first names on my list was Adam Morse—the guy who was mock arrested with me back in college. Adam and I had been friends since he moved to Northeast Wisconsin in sixth grade, and we both moved to Madison after our senior year to attend college.

"Hi Adam, it's Steve. I wanted to ask if you'd be willing to get involved in 40 Days for Life this fall."

"What's 40 Days for Life?"

In all my enthusiasm, I didn't even think to explain what the campaign was before I invited Adam. In all honesty, I didn't think he'd be interested. I wasn't sure how he felt about abortion, and I suspected he might think the idea of public prayer at an abortion center was at least a little "out there." After I finally got around to telling Adam what the campaign was, I was surprised when he decided to join our effort. I was even more surprised when Adam started committing to the 5:00 a.m. shift every day before work.

Praying alongside friends, both new and old, I learned my faith out on the sidewalk. For the first time, I was exposed to prayers like the Divine Mercy Chaplet, which has become a staple in my prayer life. But, while I grew in devotion, I learned that I still had quite a bit of room to grow in humility. My overnight vigil shifts led me to feel pretty self-satisfied. *I'm out at four o'clock in the morning; I'm a pretty good pro-lifer.* I got a hard dose of reality in the second half of the campaign when I started taking more daytime shifts at Planned Parenthood, particularly the day shifts on abortion days. It was one thing to pray with friends amidst the calmness of a crisp autumn night. It was a completely different thing to stand and witness as mother after mother entered the clinic pregnant—and emerged hours later not pregnant. To see women emerge from the clinic crying, sometimes staggering across the parking lot in physical, emotional, and spiritual agony. To witness the empty and hollow eyes of a woman who has had motherhood literally ripped away from her.

Years later, that shock has not worn off.

"It's easier to pray a million hours in the dead of night," I declared, "than one hour when the abortions are actually taking place." I had long believed that the horrors of abortion needed to be overcome by *defeating* our pro-choice opponents. Ever since I got involved in the political realm as a teenager, I hoped that resounding electoral triumphs followed by legislative victories would end abortion. I continued to believe that pro-lifers needed to sharpen our rhetorical skills so we could *win.*

With superior talking points, we would win debates. With skilled marketing, we would win the battle for public opinion. With clever strategy, we would strike the decisive blow to end abortion in America once and for all. Without realizing it, I put my faith in the plans of man rather than the plans of God.

Out on the sidewalks, my hubris melted away one lost baby at a time. If a woman was determined to have an abortion, there was simply nothing I could do to stop her. I could hold a sign directing her toward crisis pregnancy resources in town. I could even reach out with an encouraging word. And I could pray. But in the end, she would make the final decision.

I was *helpless*.

For a while, that deeply troubled me. I wanted to will these women to choose life. I wanted to block the parking lot entrance or bar the doors. I wanted to run into Planned Parenthood to proclaim the dignity of human life with words so eloquent that women would come pouring out of the building and rush toward the pregnancy center a few blocks away. I wanted to *solve* these abortion-bound women the same way I thought I could solve Jessica.

Instead, all I could do was stand and pray and allow my heart to be broken.

Over time, I began to understand that's *exactly* the way God wants it. After all, it is the Lord who declared, "My grace is sufficient for you, for power is made perfect in weakness," an affirmation that led St. Paul to declare, "I will rather boast most gladly of my weaknesses, in order that the power of Christ may dwell with me" (2 Corinthians 12:9). He also said, "Rend your hearts and not your garments" (Joel 2:13).

There's no quicker way to rend one's heart than to enter into the suffering of a woman who has just had the life of her pre-born child extinguished within her. I found that only when I quit trying to exert my own will and simply let God accomplish the work as He desires to, then—and only then—did I find success. And certainly, the Lord blessed us during our 40 Days for Life campaign.

One Thursday, early in the campaign, a middle-aged woman drove by the vigil site. As she passed, she honked the horn and proclaimed, "God Bless your efforts; you saved a baby today!" We never learned the rest of the story, but we were certainly encouraged by it.

Just days later, we were blessed again by an email from a volunteer who talked with a Planned Parenthood client who had a lot of questions. "What are you doing? Why are you doing it?" After the interrogation, the questioner, a twenty-year-old woman named Aleksandra admitted, "I'm pregnant." She was out of work, wasn't a U.S. citizen, and was a week away from becoming homeless. But the vigil participant was able to persuade the expectant mother to visit Madison's crisis pregnancy center, where she received help. "I told Aleksandra to call me anytime she wants to talk or whenever she needs help," the prayer warrior told me. "She asked for my contact information and said that she now thinks of me as her aunt."

GROWING PAINS

It didn't take me long to realize that even *helping* to lead a 40 Days for Life campaign was hard work. Early on, I was a little too content to dabble with the campaign in my free time. As the campaign director, Amy didn't have that luxury. There were nearly two thousand hour-long prayer shifts to fill, and the buck stopped with her.

Young and selfish, I didn't always make good on my commitments to help Amy with the campaign. It didn't take much to overwhelm me. One afternoon, Amy asked for a progress update on one of the tasks I had volunteered to complete. I hadn't kept up, and I melted down in the face of the pressure. "I wish I had never even heard of 40 Days for Life!" I told Laura. "I *hate* 40 Days for Life!"

Amy's generosity with her time stood in sharp contrast to my selfishness. When the campaign leadership team gathered for an evening to enjoy dinner together, Amy spent most of the evening in our host's basement, making phone calls to fill the vigil schedule. It wasn't going well, and the stress had pushed her to tears. In the last week of the campaign, Amy invited us to spend an evening enjoying a time-share her parents owned about an hour out of town. With only days left in the campaign, I hoped she'd take the opportunity to relax. Instead, while Laura, Peter, and I splashed around in the indoor water park, Amy made phone calls to fill the vigil schedule.

One of my biggest surprises when it came to volunteering for 40 Days for Life was how hard it was to fill the vigil schedule on Sundays. It's a day off of work. A day off of school. It's a day dedicated to serving the Lord, but we always struggled to keep the vigil going. A lot of that has to do with people spending the day at church and with their families, which is certainly a worthwhile way to honor the Lord's Day. It was also difficult because Wisconsin is rabid for football. Our participants' devotion to the Green Bay Packers is second only to their devotion to Jesus.

Laura and I decided to spend an hour at Planned Parenthood each Sunday afternoon to help ease the scheduling woes. Sometimes that meant missing both football *and* baseball. We spent the first Saturday of baseball season at the campus Planned Parenthood praying after my pathetic litany of excuses failed to get me off the hook. Now, we would spend the last day of the baseball season at Planned Parenthood as well.

Despite another late-season collapse, the Brewers rebounded in late September to enter the season's final day with a playoff spot on the line. I was able to catch most of Milwaukee's 162nd game before we had to leave for Planned Parenthood.

CC Sabathia, the team's ace pitcher, pitched a complete game, and star outfielder Ryan Braun hit a dramatic eighth-inning home run to defeat the rival Chicago Cubs. But that wasn't enough. The entire State of Wisconsin waited with bated breath to see whether the Florida Marlins could hold onto a late lead in a tight game against the New York Mets. If the Mets won, it would force a tiebreaker in New York to determine whether the Mets or Brewers advanced to the postseason.

With the outcome still in question, I winced as my family got in the car to head for the abortion facility. But unlike my first pro-life vigil, which I tried to forestall with a myriad of excuses, there would be no wavering and waffling this time.

I will admit, however, that I asked Adam to text me the moment the score went final so I wouldn't have to wait the entire hour to learn the Brewers' fate. I didn't need to. By the time my phone started buzzing, the sports bar down the road erupted in cheers to let me know Milwaukee was playoff-bound for the first time since 1982.

SOMETHING NEW

When day 40 finally came, we held a closing celebration and breakfast at a local church. I volunteered to give a speech to the attendees, recapping our local campaign and reminding our volunteers that, while day 40 had come and gone, our work was not done. The occasion marked the first time I had ever spoken publicly.

Around that time, Amy approached Laura and me with some news. She and Tom were planning to relocate to a new community. She needed somebody to take over leadership of 40 Days for Life. Would we be willing to replace her?

Reflecting upon Jessica and her baby, on the heartbroken man who received the cruel letter bearing the ultrasound image of his aborted child, and on each of the many pained faces we saw entering and leaving Planned Parenthood, the answer was easy. We'd be delighted to lead 40 Days for Life.

"Laura, I feel so honored that Amy asked us to take this on," I said. "It's humbling to lead this effort; it's such a blessing to be able to serve in this capacity," I continued. "But I am *really* glad that we've got an entire year before we have to take this on ourselves!"

Dedicating ourselves to 40 Days for Life was difficult. It was challenging. It was hard to be out on the sidewalk and see desperate mothers come for abortions. It was incredibly difficult to recruit volunteers to stand in unbroken vigil, two at a time, for nearly one thousand consecutive hours. The grueling campaign tests the resolve of even the most committed pro-lifer, and now it would be on our shoulders.

We wanted to get an early start. Only weeks after the campaign closed, we began meeting with Amy to work on the leadership transition. With no need to schedule any more hours, Amy could let her hair down a little at these meetings. In fact, we spent one Saturday afternoon watching the movie *Amazing Grace*. The film highlights the life of the great British statesman William Wilberforce, who overcame seemingly insurmountable political opposition and chronic illness to abolish the slave trade.

The climax of the movie occurs when Parliament finally votes to end the slave trade. Charles Fox, a fellow member of the House of Commons, hails Wilberforce's perseverance and courage:

> When people speak of great men, they think of men like Napoleon—men of violence. Rarely do they think of peaceful men. But contrast the reception they will receive when they return home from their battles. Napoleon will arrive in pomp and in power, a man who's achieved the very summit of earthly ambition. And yet his dreams will be haunted by the oppressions of war. William Wilberforce, however, will return to his family, lay his head on his pillow and remember: the slave trade is no more.[1]

Was it even possible to attain that sort of peace in a country where more than a million lives are lost to abortion annually? I wasn't sure, but I knew we needed to follow Wilberforce's example and give the fight everything we had.

5

Bleeding Badger Red

~~~

Filmmaker Woody Allen once paraphrased an old Yiddish proverb, saying, "If you want to make God laugh, tell Him your plans."[1] I think about that line every time I recall my words to Laura in November of 2008, about how grateful I was that we'd have an entire year to rest, recuperate, and prepare before we ramped up our pro-life efforts for another 40 Days for Life campaign. When I uttered those words, I imagine that the Lord must have laughed. I had no idea what was coming next, but the Lord certainly did.

I always savor the days in between Christmas and New Year's Day. After the rush of shopping and presents and food and travel, the last week of the year always provides a few days to quietly bask in the glow of our Savior's birth with family and friends.

I spent the evening of December 30 enjoying one of those sleepy December evenings with my wife and son. That is until shortly after dinner when the calm was broken by one of the strangest and most troubling phone calls I've ever received.

The number on my caller ID was from Washington, D.C. I picked up the phone, expecting a telemarketer, but the voice on the other end identified himself as an attorney named Matt Bowman. He was calling on behalf of the Alliance Defense Fund (ADF). The ADF, which was later renamed the Alliance Defending Freedom, is a Christian organization that advocates on behalf of individuals to freely live out their faith. Matt acknowledged that I didn't know him. But to establish his credibility, he informed me that we shared a number of mutual friends. Friends like Amy and like Will Goodman, a pro-life hero I met at our closing breakfast the previous month.

After exchanging pleasantries, Matt dropped the bombshell on me: a new abortion facility was being planned for Madison. I winced. We had our hands full trying to cover Planned Parenthood in prayer, and now the abortion industry was opening up a second front in the battle over human life.

As Matt continued, I learned that he had only scratched the surface of the horror beginning to unfold in Madison. Not only was a new abortion center in the works, but it would be a *late-term abortion center* led by University of Wisconsin professor Caryn Dutton.[2] And it would be located *right next to campus.*

Matt learned the news from Dr. Nancy Fredericks, a pro-life anesthesiologist. Dr. Fredericks had been called into a meeting where it was revealed that her workplace, the Madison Surgery Center, would begin performing late-term abortions. She immediately knew the decision would create chaos and unwanted controversy, but her medical director told her not to worry yet. Pro-life staff members would get to have their say. "Just don't say anything to anyone else, right now."[3]

However, while the secret plan continued to progress, the opportunity to speak up never came. "It became clear this thing was rolling forward . . . and that we are not ever going to have any meaningful input," Dr Fredericks recalled. "I got frightened."[4]

That fear led Dr. Fredericks to call Matt at the ADF. Matt told me the children targeted by the abortion center would be second-trimester babies between thirteen and twenty-three weeks old. According to the ADF, a second-trimester abortion "rips the child's arms and legs off piecemeal and pulls them out with forceps. These dismemberments are followed by the child's torso and head, the latter of which is sometimes so large that it needs to be crushed until the baby's brains are observed flowing out of the uterus."[5]

Abortions after twenty weeks' gestation are so gruesome and so brutal that they aren't legal even in most of secular Europe. In fact, fewer than ten countries allow elective abortion after twenty weeks—countries like the United States, Canada, the People's Republic of China, and North Korea.[6] When the United States finds itself on a human rights list next to China and North Korea, it's a sure sign that something has gone terribly wrong.

This news couldn't have been more devastating. Pro-lifers were already understandably anxious. The Madison Surgery Center abortion scheme was bad news, but in the context of other abortion industry gains, it was particularly deflating. In only three weeks, Barack Obama would be inaugurated as the nation's forty-fourth president. As a state senator in Illinois, Obama repeatedly opposed the Born Alive Infant Protection Act (BAIPA)—a bill designed to require medical providers to provide lifesaving treatment to children born alive following a botched abortion procedure.[7] The president-elect's position was an extreme one. Even NARAL Pro-Choice America, a leading pro-abortion lobbying organization, had no problem with the bill. A NARAL spokesperson said, "We, in fact, did not oppose the bill. There is a clear legal difference between a fetus in utero versus a child that's born. And when a child is born, they deserve every protection that the country can provide."[8] A federal version of BAIPA—nearly identical to the one Obama voted against—passed Congress with almost no opposition and was signed into law by President Bush in 2002.[9]

Obama's opposition to BAIPA was far from the only sign that the incoming administration would be dangerous for unborn children. During the campaign, he spoke about his support for educating teens on contraceptive use, saying, "I've got two daughters, 9 years old and 6 years old. I am going to teach them first of all about values and morals. But if they make a mistake, I don't want them punished with a baby."[10] The idea that a baby might be described as a *punishment* was chilling to say the least.

The most immediately troubling sign of what pro-lifers might be up against in President-Elect Obama, however, was that during his short stint in the U.S. Senate, Obama had been a co-sponsor of the euphemistically titled "Freedom of Choice Act" (FOCA). The effect of FOCA would be to override almost all state-level pro-life legislation. With the stroke of a pen, nearly every abortion restriction in America would vanish. The incoming president promised on the campaign trail, ". . . the first thing I'd do as president is, is sign the Freedom of Choice Act. That's the first thing that I'd do."[11] Various versions of FOCA had been introduced in Congress over the years, but they never stood a realistic chance of being enacted. Obama, however, was about to take office with heavy Democratic majorities in both houses of Congress.

The abortion industry was on the move. Already playing defense, it became clear that Wisconsin's pro-life community would have its hands full trying to prevent the opening of another abortion center.

LIFE IN THE MAD CITY

As an alumnus of the University of Wisconsin, the news of my alma mater's hospital opening a late-term abortion facility right next to campus hit me particularly hard. Like many Badger State natives, I grew up adoring the university. At nine years old, I found myself captivated as Wisconsin Badger coach Barry Alvarez led the team to a most unexpected Big Ten Championship in 1993. The Cinderella season was followed by the school's first Rose Bowl appearance in more than three decades. More than twenty-five years later, I still remember watching the dramatic final minutes of the game in my parents' living room as the Badgers won their first Rose Bowl in school history.

That Rose Bowl victory helped transform Wisconsin into a perennial Big Ten powerhouse and put the program on the map nationally. The Badger football program won back-to-back Rose Bowls in 1999 and 2000. Along the way, the team outdueled eventual NFL stars—including future Hall of Fame quarterback Drew Brees twice. One of the most exciting storylines involved star running back Ron Dayne breaking college football's all-time rushing record on his way to winning the Heisman Trophy.

The football team's success resonated throughout the entire university. In 2000, the men's basketball team upset several higher-ranked teams on its way to an appearance in the Final Four. Meanwhile, the men's hockey team spent much of the season ranked number one on the ice.

You didn't need to be a student or an alumnus; the entire state fell in love with the University of Wisconsin. Whether the school's accomplishments were academic, athletic, musical, or in any other field, Wisconsinites were more than happy to celebrate them. The institution was revered such that those who were students or alumni often seemed to garner a little more respect from their friends and neighbors back home where they grew up.

That's the context to my entry into the university in 2002, and my own experience did not disappoint. As a freshman, I was fortunate to win a lottery allowing me to purchase season tickets in the student section for Badger football games. The team played the season opener against Fresno State University about a week and a half before classes started. I was mesmerized.

I had been to professional sporting events before, but the amazing pageantry of the college game took the experience to the next level. The coordinated chanting from the student section, the elaborate song and dance routines in conjunction with the school marching band, and the absurd behavior in the student section represented sheer revelry. The highlight of the night was the interlude between the third and fourth quarters when the stadium sound system blared House of Pain's 1992 hit, *Jump Around*. At once, the entire student section, the band, and even some of the players began to—well—jump around, providing quite the spectacle and causing the stadium's upper deck to sway on its foundation. The atmosphere was equally delightful and vulgar. I had obviously heard the "F-bomb" dropped before. I had never heard it dropped by ten thousand people in unison toward the fans of the opposing team. For better and for worse, my first football game was a baptism of sorts. I was now a Badger.

Along with the thousands of other freshmen arriving to campus, my membership in Badger-dom became my identity. Before long, the vast majority of my clothes were red and white. My parents' car was proudly adorned with a *University of Wisconsin Parent* window decal. And when I came home for Christmas and spring break, my friends back home probably got pretty tired of hearing about how great life in Madison was.

My adopted hometown was nicknamed "The Mad City"—a well-earned moniker. In addition to the radical political atmosphere, the city was something of a petri dish of immoral behavior, even by college life standards. As one itinerant street preacher proclaimed, "It's the University of WisconSIN!"

I had a front-row seat for all of it. From my room on the top floor of the tallest high-rise dorm on campus—the penthouse suite, I called it—I could look out my window to the right and admire the dome of the beautiful state capitol or look to the left and observe noisy, drunken belligerents wandering the streets aimlessly. Life in Madison was exciting, and I loved every minute of it.

HOCKEY AND ROMANCE

Though I didn't realize it until many months later, it was my freshman orientation where I met Laura. She was from Illinois, and one of my classmates from high school introduced me to her, noting that she had never heard a particularly vulgar pejorative that Wisconsinites sometimes use to describe our neighbors to the south.

Laura's memory of me was that she found me "neurotic" as I frantically tried to determine my class schedule. Because Laura and I were at the same advising sessions and both in the honors program, we wound up in two of the same classes that first semester. Laura lived in the dorms near some of my high school classmates, so we continued to cross paths during the second semester. We were more acquaintances than friends, but when the academic year ended, I invited her to a big beginning-of-summer party I threw at my parents' house. No alcohol, just a bonfire and the opportunity to bring my old high school friends together with new college friends to kick off the summer. To my surprise, Laura accepted the invitation.

Apparently, the performance of my high school garage band impressed her—or at least she didn't find it too embarrassing—because Laura left the party thinking she might like to date me. When school resumed in the fall, she told a mutual friend named Sarah to relay that fact to me. I was pretty awkward around girls, and my most recent girlfriend was from high school. I was also quite certain Laura was out of my league, but I decided I'd ask her out to dinner anyway. After all, maybe I could learn how to date—or at least work some of the awkwardness out of my system—before Laura realized I wasn't her type and inevitably broke up with me.

I found my opportunity to ask her out on a date in less-than-romantic circumstances.

The previous spring, Sarah had dragged me to a hockey game at the Kohl Center, just across the street from my dorm. I wasn't the slightest bit interested.

"It's going to be boring!" I protested. "Who wants to sit around for a couple hours just to see one or two goals scored?"

"Just give it a try," Sarah said. "The games are a lot of fun."

Reluctantly, I acquiesced.

To my great surprise, Sarah was right. While the hockey game was low scoring, it was a lot of fun. And when the Badgers broke a 1-1 tie with a breakaway goal in the game's final minute, I was hooked.

Sarah, Laura, and a number of mutual friends bought season tickets for our sophomore year. But, in order to get good seats down near the ice, you needed to show up early when tickets went on sale—not hours early but *days* early. Our group of friends hatched a plan we called "Urban Camping." For two straight days, we'd wait out in front of the Kohl Center. The weather was already cold, so we'd need to bundle up and bring sleeping bags.

Some of the girls in our crew drew up a shift schedule so we could balance our time in line with our studies. I was slotted to spend a couple hours with Laura, so I'd have the perfect opportunity to ask her on a date. There was only one problem: one of our friends was so enthusiastic about Urban Camping that he wouldn't leave the stadium. I missed my shot. But when our shift replacements arrived, I came up with plan B.

"It's getting cold out here. Before Laura and I leave for the evening, we can go pick you up some hot chocolate."

The girls knew what I was up to and said they'd very much enjoy some hot chocolate. To my great dismay, the enthusiastic urban camper said he'd like some as well and would join us at the cafeteria. Barely concealing my anger and frustration after a largely sleepless night in the arena's front yard, I shouted through gritted teeth, "I'll bring it back for you!"

On our first date, Laura told me that she considered going into the convent and becoming a nun, but that she just couldn't do it because of how badly she felt the Catholic Church mistreats women. Given Laura's great fidelity to the Church today, this remark amuses me not a little.

Our second date took us to the Memorial Union. Probably the most beautiful venue in town, the student union features a waterfront terrace with scenic views of both the capitol and Lake Mendota. On weekends when the weather is nice, hundreds of people come out to sit on the terrace and listen to live music—an experience magnified by the sights of sailboats on the water, the smell of brats on the grill, and the taste of the union's famous ice cream made at the dairy right on campus.

The weather for our second date that October night was unseasonably warm, so the terrace was packed. Laura and I wanted to get away from the noise, and we strolled down the lakefront until we came to the second-to-last pier on the lake. From our spot at the end of the pier, we could still see the festivities at the union on the horizon, but we were far enough out that the roar of the crowd was now a mere hum. Under the moon and the stars and with the capitol dome towering in the distance, we sat and talked for hours. About life. About death. About our families. We talked about our hopes and dreams for the future. We fell in love.

As a political science major, I began to feel that my course of study wasn't the most rigorous or practical. Laura was double majoring in Spanish and international studies and ultimately graduated with honors, earning *A*s in every course but one. I thought I might do well to step up my game. I rather enjoyed the intro-level journalism class I took to fulfill my gen-ed requirements and decided to apply for the School of Journalism, if for no other reason than that it might impress Laura. The journalism school was ranked in the top ten in the nation and was incredibly competitive. Only one hundred students would get in—most of them juniors. I was only a sophomore.

Nevertheless, I compiled my transcripts, gathered my letters of recommendation, and went to the J-School office to submit my application. I arrived at 3:00 p.m., took one last look at my application, and realized the deadline was at noon. "NO EXCEPTIONS," the form read.

Devastated, I headed back to my dorm. Later that afternoon, I told Laura of my plight, and she urged me to give it one last shot. "'No exceptions' doesn't always mean 'no exceptions,'" she said. I told her it was futile, but she insisted. I relented and called the J-School office. If I could get the application in by 5:00 p.m., they'd take it.

I was running out of time, and the J-School was about a thirty-minute walk from my dorm. Laura dropped by to lend me her bike. She's rather diminutive in stature, so I must have looked ridiculous, peddling across campus with my knees pumping up to my ears. But I beat the clock and a month later learned I had been granted admittance to the University of Wisconsin School of Journalism and Mass Communication.

The end of the fall semester loomed like a dark cloud over our relationship. In January, Laura would move to Ecuador for a semester to study Spanish. Our time apart was difficult. Laura's access to the telephone and to the internet was intermittent at best. We sometimes went weeks without speaking, and when we did speak, a delay on the line made conversation difficult. Limited by her sporadic access to internet cafes, her emails often consisted of just a few short sentences.

In retrospect, the lack of communication might have been a good thing—at least for my peace of mind. On her first day in Quito, Laura was abandoned by her host brother without an address to which she could return. Only a tearful visit to the International Student Office helped her find "home." Even more disturbingly, one of Laura's longer emails revealed that Laura was considering participating in a class experience involving the use of hallucinogenic drugs as part of an indigenous witchcraft ritual. Laura wasn't just opposed to drugs; she was a complete teetotaler. But for my little moral relativist, even hard drug use and sorcery could be justified as a cultural experience. I ended up persuading Laura to not participate, which might have saved our relationship.

By the time Laura returned home that May, I became increasingly convinced that I wanted to marry her. Laura wasn't so sure. Not yet, at least. I wasn't looking for a firm commitment right away, but I did want to know whether she thought there was a chance that her future might involve me. If not, we were both wasting our time.

I hassled Laura for about six months without really getting anywhere. When Laura took me out for a fancy French dinner on my twenty-first birthday, I continued my interrogation. Though she had hoped to save the news until Christmas, I had finally worn her down. "I'm ready," she said. "I'll marry you."

I was merely hoping to discuss the possibility; I wasn't expecting a commitment! But Laura had thought about it and she'd made up her mind. Two months later, we returned to our pier on the lakefront near the student union, and I got down on a knee to propose.

Laura and I married the month after graduation. Laura donned a Bucky Badger garter under her dress, and when the band took a break at our reception, we played a CD of the University of Wisconsin Marching Band. The dance floor remained full as fellow alumni joined the choreographed dances that every current or former student knows by heart.

I couldn't wait for the two of us to enter the real world and make our mark on it as Badger alumni. We continued to attend Wisconsin sporting events and visit the Memorial Union Terrace. We decked out our apartment with Badger paraphernalia. And the very first outfit we bought for Peter after learning Laura was pregnant was a Badger onesie. The University of Wisconsin was our home, the place where we met and fell in love, the backdrop for the greatest moments of our lives. We bled Badger red.

But bleeding Badger red was about to take on a very different meaning.

6

Revealing the Secret

∿

As I began to grasp what the University of Wisconsin's late-term abortion scheme meant, Matt Bowman continued to share with me the troubling implications. The abortions would be performed at the Madison Surgery Center—an outpatient surgery center co-owned and run by the University of Wisconsin Hospital and Clinics (UWHC), the University of Wisconsin Medical Foundation, and Meriter Hospital.[1] Ironically, the Madison Surgery Center was located across the street from Meriter's state-of-the-art neonatal center. On one side of the street, physicians would strive to save the lives of premature babies. On the other side, they would dismember babies about the same age. The participation of University of Wisconsin physicians made it possible that a state ban on public funding for abortion would be violated.[2]

Long before David Daleiden and the Center for Medical Progress exposed Planned Parenthood's practice of selling body parts harvested from aborted babies, pro-lifers knew the university had long been engaged in research on fetal tissue procured during abortions. Open-records requests later documented a UW study that involved transplanting pancreas tissue harvested from aborted babies into diabetes patients.[3] Matt told me that it was quite likely that the university wanted to establish the late-term abortion center, in part, to provide a cheaper source of fetal body parts. This revelation probably should not have been a surprise. The school had a history of pioneering medical research offensive to the dignity of human life. Ten years earlier, University of Wisconsin scientist Dr. James Thomson became the first researcher to successfully isolate and culture stem cells harvested through the destruction of human embryos.[4]

Finally, Matt told me that the Madison Surgery Center abortion plan would likely force pro-life medical personnel to assist with the gruesome late-term abortions, violating their conscience rights and breaking conscience protection laws in the process.

Initially, Matt's client, Dr. Nancy Fredericks wasn't so sure the situation would devolve the way Matt predicted. She trusted in her department's promise that pro-life employees would be scheduled so that they wouldn't have to assist. She understood the hollowness of this reassurance only after Matt asked her a horrifying question: "Do you really think . . . that people who have no qualms about taking innocent, pre-born life will have any qualms about trampling on your conscience rights?"[5] Furthermore, botched abortions—and there would be botched abortions—don't follow a shift schedule. Whoever was on duty would be required to participate.

Matt told me he was sharing these shocking developments with me because he had learned that I recently took over leadership of Madison's 40 Days for Life campaign and he wanted my help in fighting this plan.

"Absolutely," I said. "But what can I do?"

Matt said that the Madison Surgery Center was deliberately keeping its late-term abortion scheme secret to prevent any sort of public backlash or outcry. In fact, letters recovered from an open-records request revealed the lengths to which officials went to hide the plan. For example, Madison Surgery Center Administrative Director Cheryl Wilson wrote to UW Medical Foundation Executive Vice President and COO Peter Christman, "We preferred to meet at 20 S. Park St. instead of 1 S. Park St. [the address of the Madison Surgery Center] so MSC staff did not see us meeting and inquire about the reason for the meeting."[6]

But the secrecy was about to come to an abrupt end.

Within a week, Matt and the ADF were going to issue a major announcement exposing the plan. Pro-Life Wisconsin would follow with an announcement of its own, condemning the plan and urging the public to register its opposition.

Matt asked whether I was familiar with the pro-life response to the abortion megacenter that had opened in Aurora. Of course, I was; I had lived there when it happened. It was my first exposure to 40 Days for Life. Matt wanted to replicate the efforts of the Pro-Life Action League and the 40 Days for Life team in Aurora to keep late-term abortion out of the University of Wisconsin. He asked me to rally our local 40 Days for Life team for a peaceful, pro-life demonstration in front of the Madison Surgery Center within a day or two of his announcement.

"Sure," I said. But I was worried about our ability to turn out a crowd on short notice. "What is the minimum number of people we should have there to make sure our presence isn't an embarrassment?"

"Do you think you can get twenty or twenty-five people there?"

"I think so. I'll do my best."

I was about to ask some more questions, but Matt was running out of time. He asked me to keep everything confidential because it was important that his announcement the following week catch by surprise the Madison Surgery Center and the three institutions that own it. I couldn't tell anybody about our conversation. He ended the call saying, "I can't talk anymore right now, but I know you're having lunch with [Pro-Life Wisconsin's] Matt Sande tomorrow. He'll fill you in on everything else you need to know."

Just as suddenly as Matt's call broke the silence of a quiet, late-December night, it was over. I hung up and told Laura, "That was probably the strangest call I've ever received."

WE CAN'T TALK ABOUT IT HERE

The next day, I met Matt Sande at a local pizza place for lunch. We hadn't even ordered our meal yet, but the suspense was killing me.

"Matt, so this other Matt," I started, "Matt Bowman, called me last night . . ."

My friend knew where the conversation was headed and looked nervous, scanning the room to see whether anybody else in the pizzeria might be eavesdropping.

". . . and he said there's going to be a new abortion center in Madison, and he wants me to help him try to stop it from opening. He told me to talk to you about it at lunch today."

Matt covered his mouth with the menu, lowered his voice, and replied, "We can talk about this, Steve. We can definitely talk about this. But we can't talk about it *here*. After we eat, we'll go out to the car, and I'll give you the details."

I felt like I had unwittingly been dropped into the script of a Hollywood blockbuster action film. Matt and I had plenty of topics for conversation, but the moment I finished my pepperoni flatbread and paid the bill, it was off to my car to find out what was going on.

For years, a local physician named Dennis Christiansen operated the Madison Abortion Clinic.[7] Christiansen had performed tens of thousands of abortions[8] at facilities across the Midwest,[9] ultimately locating his private practice at a new abortion facility opened by Planned Parenthood[10] in 2004.[11] However, now Christiansen was retiring.[12] Planned Parenthood would take on the first-trimester abortions, and the decision was made to move the late-term abortions to the Madison Surgery Center. University of Wisconsin professor and Planned Parenthood Associate Medical Director Dr. Caryn Dutton would perform the abortions[13] at a facility adjacent to the college campus.

We later learned that Christiansen didn't retire after all. Before long, he was spotted working at abortion facilities in Milwaukee.[14] Planned Parenthood began providing abortions without his assistance, but its practitioners apparently weren't trusted to take on the much more dangerous late-term abortions. As Dutton wrote, "[Planned Parenthood] Federation of America's confidence in our ab[ortion] service provision was very LOW."[15]

That left the Madison Surgery Center as a desirable location because it was in close proximity to both the UW Hospital and Meriter Hospital. Direct access to a hospital would come in handy when abortions were botched. And, again, abortions *would* be botched.

There was another ideological motive to performing abortions in the university health system. Leaders in the abortion industry saw an opportunity to mainstream abortion. For years, abortion advocates had been trying to claim that abortion was health care. The assertion never really took root, perhaps because Americans intuitively recognize that health care means preserving and restoring the proper functioning of the human body rather than breaking it and ending lives.

Furthermore, when abortion is isolated at stand-alone abortion clinics like Planned Parenthood, abortion centers become lightning rods for criticism and activism. By performing abortions in multipurpose surgical centers, abortion supporters felt they'd be able to remove the stigma that accompanies the killing of pre-born children.

"It is my very strong feeling that we need to safeguard hospital base [sic] abortion practices," wrote Fredrik Broekhuizen, the abortion provider at the Milwaukee Planned Parenthood, in a November 22, 2008, email to Dutton. "I really think the Madison physician community should step up to the plate as advocates . . . . If Madisonians consider themselves so progressive . . . why can't they do this . . . ?"[16]

Abortion supporters also knew mainstreaming abortion would hamper pro-life vigils, protests, and sidewalk counseling efforts. It's relatively easy to reach out to abortion-minded women at Planned Parenthood. It wouldn't be quite so easy to figure out which Madison Surgery Center patients were coming for abortions and which were coming for dermatology appointments on another floor.

While it took time to learn the abortion industry's true motives, my conversations with both Matt Sande and Matt Bowman gave me a solid understanding of what we were up against. And now it was time for me to figure out how I was going to assemble a crowd in front of this would-be abortion center. I wasn't sure it could be done. How does one rally the pro-life community on only forty-eight hours' notice? On a workday? A school day? And at a location with very little public parking? And as if those challenges weren't enough to contend with, it would be the second week of January in Wisconsin!

My first order of business was to send out a save-the-date email to our volunteer list, which included hundreds of pro-lifers in the area. But I still didn't have the green light to share the news that the university health system was looking to open an abortion clinic. I worried that without specific details, our email would be ignored. Matt Sande's wife Rebecca suggested that our vagueness might have the opposite effect. Perhaps, we'd be able to build intrigue. We gave it a shot. I blasted our volunteers with a simple message:

A MAJOR pro-life event will be held around the downtown area on Thursday, January 8 at 8:00 a.m. Unfortunately, at this time we are not able to disclose exactly what and where this event will be, but please trust us: it will be crucial to the pro-life movement in Madison.

We will be able to deliver all the details on Tuesday in a special Vigil for Life email. Until then, we ask that if you are able, please block off the 8:00 a.m. hour to attend this event. Certainly, many of you will be working or otherwise engaged. If this is the case, please let your pro-life friends and family members know. And please pray for the success of the event.

BLOWING THE LID OFF

My note succeeded at creating a buzz amidst the pro-life community in Madison. That buzz continued to grow Tuesday morning, January 6, when the ADF issued its announcement blowing the lid off the Madison Surgery Center abortion scheme. "Pro-life employees shouldn't be forced to violate their conscience by participating in the killing of preborn, developed babies," the statement quoted Bowman as saying. "The university's plan is morally and legally flawed and should be abandoned."[17]

Pro-Life Wisconsin followed up an hour later with a release of its own. "Pro-Life Wisconsin condemns the UWHC/Meriter Hospital plan to do late-term abortions at the Madison Surgery Center," wrote State Director Peggy Hamill. "We are appalled to learn that our . . . University of Wisconsin hospital and medical foundation is planning to directly participate in the dismemberment of second-trimester babies, babies that can suck their thumbs, turn somersaults in their mother's wombs, and whose hearts are pumping gallons of blood every day."[18]

Two hours later, Vigil for Life (the organization that leads 40 Days for Life in Madison) issued a news release of our own, condemning the abortion plan and reissuing the invitation to attend the peaceful demonstration we scheduled for January 8. In the announcement, I couldn't help but to point out the significance I found in the news breaking on January 6. The secret late-term plans were revealed on Epiphany, the Christian holiday commemorating the three wise men's visit to the infant Jesus. Shortly after that visit, King Herod began his Slaughter of the Innocents, killing all of the male babies in Bethlehem.

The nearly simultaneous announcements from the ADF, Pro-Life Wisconsin, and Vigil for Life made front-page headlines immediately. Pro-lifers around the state demanded answers. Even Wisconsin's congressional delegation took notice with future Speaker of the House Paul Ryan and Rep. James Sensenbrenner denouncing the plan.[19] Sen. Glenn Grothman and Rep. Rich Zipperer headlined a list of more than forty state legislators in signing a letter urging the abandonment of the late-term abortion plan.[20]

Meanwhile, UWHC staff members were caught completely flat-footed. As the story generated front-page headlines, UWHC struggled to justify the dismemberment of pre-born children—even to a community as liberal as Madison. "The physicians believe that there is a public health responsibility to provide [abortion] as part of comprehensive reproductive health care," UWHC spokesperson Lisa Brunette said.[21]

UWHC's justification of the abortion plan focused on rare cases, when expectant mothers faced a challenging health condition or when their babies had been diagnosed with a serious disability late in pregnancy. There seemed to be an implicit assumption that, of course, we should abort the babies with disabilities. The real question was whether they could get away with aborting the healthy ones, too. In any case, internal emails revealed that three quarters of late-term abortions are entirely elective.[22] Brunette admitted that publicly paid medical staff would be performing the abortions, but she rationalized it by saying that staff members would be paid by patient fees and private insurance instead of tax dollars.[23] UWHC also confirmed that it was possible that body parts harvested from aborted babies might be used in UW research projects but, according to Brunette, only after review by a faculty committee.[24] As though *that* somehow made everything ok!

UWHC also faced a serious internal public relations crisis—and one that was not unexpected. As early as November, Caryn Dutton herself knew the abortion plan would be unpopular among Madison Surgery Center staff. An email to Broekhuizen stated, "Other specialties and departments are terrified of having abortion happening in their 'space.'"[25] Dr. Fredericks publicly stated that three of the center's four anesthesiologists would refuse to participate in the abortions.[26]

A joint email from UWHC and UW Medical Foundation leadership tried to make the late-term abortion case to staff members:

> Without local availability, Madison-area women will be forced to travel to obtain this service, and may obtain the service under conditions that are less than optimal. The concerned physicians who brought this issue forward and many UW Health and Meriter leaders believe there is public-health responsibility to provide these procedures as part of comprehensive program of family planning and reproductive health care.[27]

The email also featured one other piece of information that proved *extremely* useful: "UWHC plans to discuss the [provision of second-trimester abortions] with its Board of Directors at its February board meeting."[28] This gave us a timeline. While the UW Medical Foundation and Meriter Hospital had already approved the late-term abortion plan, UWHC had not. With the board meeting coming up in February, we had about a month to persuade the board directors to abandon its plan.

7

Shock Jocks and Subzero Temperatures

~~~

The next morning, I was up early. Peter was approaching his second birthday, and he occasionally decided he was ready for breakfast long before Laura or I were ready to get out of bed. Still trying to get my bearings, I got him in his highchair and staggered into the kitchen to grab him a cereal bar. That's when the phone rang. I didn't recognize the number. Who could be calling this early?

"Hello, this is Steve—"

At this point in my life, I wasn't really a morning person and I've never been a coffee drinker, so I was still trying to shake the cobwebs out. The voice at the other end of the line was talking so quickly as she introduced herself that I had no idea with whom I was speaking.

"Are you the one organizing the anti-abortion event tomorrow?"

"Yes, I am," I responded.

"Do you have any time to talk about it?"

"Yes."

"Do you have time *right now?*"

"Uh . . . sure?"

The next thing I heard was, "We're joined now, live, by Steve Karlen of Madison Vigil for Life . . . "

I had just gotten out of bed. The sun wasn't up. I was still half asleep. And now I was on live radio discussing abortion with no idea whose program I was on nor what the host's agenda was.

It turns out I was discussing the Madison Surgery Center late-term abortion plan with John Sylvester—also known as the notorious Madison morning shock jock, "Sly in the Morning." At the time, I didn't know much about him, but I developed a pretty good idea of what he was about when he said something to the effect of, "I'm sure nobody would have been too upset if George W. Bush's mom had gotten a vacuum job."

Sly grilled me for about fifteen minutes on the topic of late-term abortion. By the grace of God, I held up well, keeping my composure in the midst of what felt like an ambush. And in doing so, I was able to provide him and his listeners with the truth about the brutality of late-term abortion and the humanity of the pre-born child. Certainly, I didn't manage to persuade Sly to become a staunch pro-lifer, but—to his credit—he was receptive to what I had to say. He was openly stunned to learn that the babies who would be aborted at the Madison Surgery Center were developed enough that their mothers could feel their kicks.

I got off the call, took a deep breath, and listened to a caller affirm that, yes, as a mother she could feel her baby kick around twenty weeks into her pregnancy. Nevertheless, in the eyes of the caller, that wasn't enough to warrant protection for the pre-born child; she affirmed that decisions about abortion should be made "not by some guy who's read about abortion" but by a woman and her doctor.

Still, the interview was a success. The mainstream media love to ignore the abortion issue, but I had just gone on one of the local media's most liberal talk shows and discussed fetal development. This was a victory.

It was also a personal victory as I realized that I'd never again face a media interview as difficult as my fifteen-minute interrogation by a leftist talk-show host. Later in the day, I fielded another interview with a radio station across the state. Still slightly shaken by my discussion with Sly, I approached the interview cautiously; that is, until about halfway through the conversation when I realized that I was appearing on a Christian program!

As it turns out, this wasn't my last interaction with Sly. A year or two later, I attended the benefit dinner of a local pro-life pregnancy help organization. To my great surprise, one of the board members introduced me to Sly in the flesh. She told me he was moved by the Catholic Church's commitment to the poor and converted to the faith. All conversions are works in progress, and I don't know whether he now considers himself pro-life, pro-choice, or somewhere in between. But to see him attending the fundraising banquet for a pro-life pregnancy center was more than a little rewarding—especially considering his "vacuum job" remark.

When I thanked Sly for having me on his program, he thought for a moment before a lightbulb went on and he said, "Oh! Yeah! You did a good job."

THE PROTEST

To say I was nervous as I woke up the morning of our demonstration in front of the Madison Surgery Center would be an understatement. Our goal was twenty-five people on the streets, but when the windchills dropped far below zero, I began to wonder whether anybody would show up.

After leaving Peter with a babysitter, I arrived at the site without much time to spare and was relieved to see a couple dozen people already assembled. With the wind picking up, I greeted the attendees personally to thank them for coming. As the clock struck eight, and our event officially started, the crowd had grown by a few dozen. And, by the time everybody found parking, hundreds of pro-lifers had gathered on the sidewalk.

In the midst of all the excitement, I forgot to dress appropriately for the weather. A rally attendee named David Stiennon offered me a winter hat and a pair of gloves.

"No thank you," I replied. "I'll be ok."

His sharp rebuke caught me by surprise.

"No, you won't! Take them!"

I obliged.

To open the demonstration in prayer, we had invited Father Rick Heilman. I first met Fr. Heilman about six months earlier, but he was well known in the pro-life community as the founder of the Knights of Divine Mercy—a Catholic men's group that could be counted on for ground support whenever the faith, the family, or human life were under attack. After being appointed pastor at a church in a little town named Pine Bluff, Wisconsin, Fr. Heilman was outraged by a strip club that opened across the street from his small country parish. He rallied his parishioners to walk and pray in front of the establishment, which they did nearly around-the-clock. Within six months, the strip club closed.[1] When the building reopened under new ownership as a legitimate bar and grill, Fr. Heilman began hosting dinner following the monthly Knights of Divine Mercy meetings in the establishment's banquet hall. At one of my first Knights of Divine Mercy meetings, Fr. Heilman proudly showed me where he was told the pole the dancers used had been.

After Fr. Heilman opened us in prayer, it was my turn to speak—only the second time I had ever spoken in public. I began by noting that—even with forty-eight hours to respond to the ADF's allegations on the potential illegality of the late-term abortion plans—neither UW nor Meriter Hospital had provided any meaningful answers. Two days had now passed since Matt Bowman and Wisconsin's pro-life community raised some serious questions for Meriter and UW officials. How would the university abide by a multitude of laws prohibiting public money from financing abortion? Would pro-life health-care workers be forced to participate? And was the university planning to harvest organs from the babies they aborted? I then chided UW and Meriter Hospital for their lack of transparency, adding, "If the UW Hospital and Clinics intended to be forthcoming and transparent, as we should expect from a public institution, we'd have answers by now. But still we wait. Shame on you, UW, and shame on you, Meriter!"

Both literally and figuratively, the gloves were off. I needed to remove my gloves so that I could hold the notes I compiled for my statement, and by the time my seven minutes with the megaphone were up, I was glad David had insisted I use his gloves. My hands were tingling, and I was beginning to lose feeling in them.

But the freezing cold weather couldn't put a damper on the day. Our event was a complete success. Hundreds of people stood in peaceful witness all up and down the street—both sides of the street—and wrapped around the corner on one of the area's busiest thoroughfares at eight o'clock in the morning. And, though the demonstration was scheduled for only sixty minutes, it was still going strong more than two hours later. Our pro-life prayer warriors had come, and they had come with determination. The subzero windchill merely strengthened their resolve as they sang, prayed, praised God, and bore witness to the sanctity of human life.

On top of all that, the media was out in force. Our event was the headline story in the city newspapers. Matt Sande and I conducted on-site interviews that were replayed on radio stations across the state, and the demonstration was the lead story on the evening news. The message was clear: the pro-life community would not accept the installation of a late-term abortion center at our beloved university's health system sitting down.

IN IT TO WIN IT

By the end of the event, I couldn't wait to get on the phone and share with out-of-town friends and family members what the Lord had accomplished in Madison that morning. And, it was with great exuberance that Laura and I settled in to watch the evening news broadcasts cover the demonstration. But as the evening turned to night and the news credits rolled, my mood began to change. I grew somber. After Laura and I put Peter to bed, I walked out of his room, sat down in the hallway, buried my head in my hands, and began to cry.

"What's wrong?" Laura asked.

I didn't know how to respond so I feebly muttered, "It's a game."

"What do you mean?"

We held a big rally. Hundreds of people came. We were in the news all over the state of Wisconsin. With a big controversy unfolding, we had done our part, and the media had done theirs. But in a day or two, the late-term abortion scheme would be old news, and the television affiliates would go back to stock market reports and basketball scores.

One memory from the day left me particularly haunted. When I arrived at the demonstration and welcomed the two dozen or so people who beat me to the rally site, I was greeted by a young girl, probably about six years old. "Hi!" she said to me before breaking into the biggest smile I've ever seen. Her smile warmed my heart. I think that little girl's smile warmed a lot of hearts that very cold day.

So why in the world was I so haunted by the memory of a beautiful little girl's smiling face? It's because, in spite of how bundled up she was for the weather, I quickly recognized that my young friend had Down syndrome. I reflected upon the fact that in the United States, the majority of children diagnosed in the womb with Down syndrome lose their lives to abortion. In many countries, that number approaches 90 percent. (An infamous CBS News report claimed Iceland is on the brink of eradicating Down syndrome—by eradicating those who have it.)[2] My young friend had made it. But I couldn't help but to think that for every beautiful, smiling face like hers, there were nine more that should be with us but are not. Once again, the crisis of abortion hit home.

As I reflected on that precious face, I found myself face-to-face with the tragic reality of abortion. I realized the one-day media spectacle would fade. So, too, did my exuberance fade with the realization that business would go back to usual. The abortion industry was content to wait us out and continue to wage war on mothers in crises and their babies—especially those with disabilities, like that beautiful little girl on the sidewalk that day.

It became exceedingly clear that we couldn't rest on the laurels of our successful demonstration. We were in it for the long haul.

8

The Giant Awakens

~~~

Because of the demonstration's success, Matt Bowman scheduled a conference call the next day with pro-life and Christian leaders throughout the state. Matt Sande, a representative from Wisconsin Right to Life, Julaine Appling of the Wisconsin Family Network, State Senator Glenn Grothman (now a congressman), and others joined the line to plan the next steps.

After reviewing the successful demonstration, we decided on the next appropriate steps to take to keep the pressure on the university health system. Various groups decided to run newspaper ads. In particular, Wisconsin Right to Life ran a brilliant half-page ad in the *State Journal* directed toward Madison Surgery Center employees. The ad featured a compelling list of reasons medical professionals would want to opt out of participating in a late-term abortion:

> Your employer has approved a late-term dismemberment abortion plan. It's time you learned

about the emotional impact of abortions on those who participate in them.

- Having to view the body parts of aborted babies
- Remembering images that cannot be shaken
- Recurring dreams and nightmares
- Withdrawal from colleagues
- Depression, fatigue, anger[1]

The ad included practical advice for Madison Surgery Center staff: "All employees have the legal right to refuse to participate in abortions. You must sign a legal form allowing you to opt out and submit it to your supervisor." It closed with a website providing such a form.

The ad created a stir, forcing UW Medical Foundation Executive Vice President and COO Peter Christman to respond to employees. Shockingly, Christman's letter admitted that staff members might be forced to participate in the late-term abortions. "The ad implies coercion of employees to assist in an emergency following an abortion," he explained. "That rare circumstance would be no different from assistance in emergencies resulting from activities such as drunk driving or drug/alcohol abuse, when health care professionals of course administer treatment despite their personal views of the reason for injury."[2]

Meanwhile, I joined fellow University of Wisconsin "Alumni for Life" in signing a letter to the *Badger Herald* that, in part, stated, "Abortion is never a service—to women, to families or the community. Certainly, abortion is not a service to the innocent pre-born baby who loses his or her life in such a violent manner."[3]

All the groups on the conference call agreed to collect petitions from around the state.

Meriter heart surgeon Dr. Bill Evans—now Fr. Bill Evans—rallied the pro-life medical community to oppose the abortion plan, saying, "There is a core group of physicians who really felt that the Madison Surgery Center is a place for healing, care and the bettering of health, and should not engage in this barbaric procedure."[4] He and a fellow specialist physician met with Meriter leadership to express their disgust that the same organization that operates a state-of-the-art neonatal facility would open an abortion center across the street. "We expected some degree of sympathy toward our position going into the meeting," Fr. Evans said looking back. "But we left that meeting knowing that our effort was thoroughly in vain and that Meriter leadership was either unwilling or unable to oppose the project in any way."

Meanwhile, Senator Grothman led twenty-nine state legislators in denouncing the abortion plan.[5] We also continued to direct phone calls to the leaders of UWHC, the UW Medical Foundation, and Meriter Hospital.

Senator Grothman suggested we host another rally—this time right in the heart of campus on a Saturday when work and school schedules would help ensure a large turnout. Because Vigil for Life had demonstrated its ability to put boots on the ground the previous day as well as through two straight around-the-clock 40 Days for Life vigils, I was tasked with organizing the rally. With the UWHC Authority Board set to vote the first week of February, we settled on Saturday, January 30. I had three weeks to pull it off.

We decided we'd hold the rally on Library Mall, a highly visible corridor on campus, named because one side of the thoroughfare included the entrance to the largest of the university's libraries. The site served as the entryway to State

Street, the high-traffic street loaded with restaurants, bars, and specialty shops. State Street also bridged the university to the state capitol building. After our rally, we would march to the Madison Surgery Center where we would hold an hour-long demonstration.

My most immediate task was to secure both a sound amplification permit for the rally as well as a parade permit for our march. The City of Madison required an attendance estimate. How could I even begin to venture a guess as to how many people would show up? We used our demonstration as a baseline, assumed that we'd have more pro-lifers available on a weekend, and put four hundred on the application. The permits also depended on the approval of the city, but I wasn't sure whether city officials would meet in time to approve our request. Fortunately, both permits came through without incident.

My next order of business was to find a powerful speaker capable of both drawing a crowd and moving the attendees to action. It wouldn't be an easy task. Airfare certainly would be expensive with such little notice. Moreover, the anniversary of the *Roe v. Wade* Supreme Court decision that legalized abortion was January 22, and pro-life speakers would be in high demand. Finally, the annual March for Life in Washington, D.C., was just before our rally, so I knew January would be a hard time to even connect with the best pro-life speakers.

Matt Bowman suggested I reach out to 40 Days for Life cofounder and national director David Bereit. Unfortunately, David was already booked that day. But he said maybe Shawn Carney could come.

Shawn was David's colleague and the other cofounder of 40 Days for Life. I connected with him by phone, explained the gravity of the situation in Madison, and asked him to provide the keynote address at our rally. After checking his schedule, he delivered me the good news: not only would Shawn headline the rally, but he'd also bring his friend, Dr. Haywood Robinson. Dr. Robinson and his wife Noreen were former abortion providers with beautiful conversion testimonies. To have both Dr. Robinson and Shawn join us for the event was truly an answer to prayer.

The controversy stayed hot throughout the month of January. On January 28, the coalition of pro-life groups that Matt Bowman brought together on the January 9 conference call held a press conference at the capitol announcing the collection of more than sixty thousand petitions opposing the university health system's late-term abortion scheme.[6] In addition to the petitions, Dr. Evans presented a letter signed by pro-life physicians in the community, which included, "Today, this group of doctors declares we can be silent no more . . . . Our vocation, our mandate, is to protect human life."[7]

Though Vigil for Life was a small group, only a year old, and a local rather than statewide group, I was proud that we had contributed more than one thousand signatures to those boxes. As we presented those signatures, I spoke to the media with a reminder that a new, unique, and individual human life begins at the moment of conception—a fact proven by both logic and empirical science. Therefore, I argued, the debate over plans to perform late-term abortions at the Madison Surgery Center is not a debate over when life begins but over which human beings we as a society decide to value and which we decide to discard. I closed by joining the growing chorus of voices calling for a boycott of both UWHC and Meriter Hospital.

Still, neither medical executives nor members of the media seemed to get it. "I was amazed at the blank stares from the journalists present," Dr. Evans said. "They could not grasp the diabolical irony of furiously working to save babies on one side of the street while exterminating them on the other."

THE RALLY

Temperatures remained frigid when Shawn and Dr. Robinson arrived the evening of Friday, January 29. Because the rally came together quickly, travel options were limited. Their journey to Wisconsin involved a series of airport layovers throughout the country, and—to hear Shawn tell the story—Dr. Robinson didn't even know where they were headed when he got to the airport the morning before the rally.

When the plane landed in Madison, the flight attendant opened the door, and an arctic blast of cold, dry January air hit the cabin. Dr. Robinson looked at Shawn nervously. "Is this our final destination?" Shawn could only laugh.

I spent the entire week excited about retrieving our guests from the airport. Given my enthusiasm for our mission, meeting Shawn and Dr. Robinson felt like the pro-life equivalent of spending time with Michael Jordan or the Beatles in their heyday. We even lined up some friends to watch Peter for a couple hours. It might have been the first time in history that providing an airport shuttle counted as a legitimate date night.

Given our age and my employment situation, finances were tight. But we splurged to get the car washed so we could make a good impression on our visitors. Once we picked up Shawn and Dr. Robinson, we made what must have seemed like an absurd invitation to a couple of freezing Texans. We invited them out for ice cream. (Wisconsin is the Dairy State after all!)

The next morning, I arrived at Library Mall early with a team of volunteers to set up. We had a stage to build, banners to hang, and a sound system to set up. My skill set was more in planning the event program rather than handling the day-of details. Fortunately, some of my co-organizers proved to be logistical geniuses and made sure the details didn't derail the event.

After a few hours of hard work, we finished setting up. There was still about an hour to go before the noon start time. The weather was starting to warm up, eventually climbing above freezing. But the long run of frostbite-inducing temperatures was replaced by a biting wind that ensured we were just as uncomfortable as we would have been had the temperatures stayed cold. In fact, photos of the event show banners that were severely scuffed up— even missing lettering. One viewing those photos might ask why we used such battered signage for a critical event. The truth is that the banners actually looked great when they were hung. The severe wind, however, kept the signs rattling all afternoon, and after a couple hours, the letters rubbed right off!

With the hard work behind us, I started to worry about attendance. Some participants had already begun to assemble, but how many would be willing to brave the winter wind? Would all our hard work be for naught? For the next forty-five minutes, I sequestered myself in the basement of a nearby church that had agreed to host us. It was the only way I could keep from spending the better part of an hour analyzing and fretting about the size of the crowd as everyone arrived.

Fifteen minutes before noon, I emerged from my refuge to make my way toward the stage. Would there be enough people on hand to send a message to UWHC administrators?

It didn't take long for me to find indicators that we were about to have a *very* good day. Before I even left the church, I met a number of attendees who had come inside to seek shelter from the elements. I greeted them and asked from where they had come.

"Wausau," the first group replied.

Wausau! I thought. These folks drove two and half hours for the event.

"We came from Iowa," the next group told me.

Sure enough, as I approached the stage, I saw Library Mall filling with pro-lifers.

"Are you the organizer?" one man asked.

"I'm one of them," I replied.

"Where is there parking for buses?"

By the time our faithful pro-lifers found parking—whether for cars or buses—we saw thousands of people converge upon Madison, Wisconsin. With the state capitol as the backdrop, pro-lifers packed Library Mall shoulder-to-shoulder for what I was later told was the biggest pro-life event the state had seen in decades.

Those pro-lifers were in for a treat. I doubt another occasion in the history of Wisconsin's pro-life movement featured so many of the state's pro-life leaders on the same stage. Fr. Rick Heilman was back, representing the Diocese of Madison, and led us in prayer. Dr. Bill Evans, who had been courageously leading the response of pro-life members of the medical community, spoke. Senator Grothman spoke on behalf of pro-life legislators. Representatives from Pro-Life Wisconsin, Wisconsin Family Council, and Wisconsin Right to Life gave brief speeches. ADF's Matt Bowman had flown in from Washington.

Laura emceed the event. At just under five feet tall, she struggled to reach the microphone. I wrapped her up in a big bear hug and lifted her up to it. The crowd erupted in laughter while somebody helped position the microphone.

As the rally's lead organizer, I had the privilege of offering the opening remarks. I began by tying our efforts in Madison to the pro-life resistance that was growing across the country. "I think the events of the last month have awakened a pro-life giant in America. [We] saw it last week in Washington [at the annual March for Life]," I said. "We said 'no' to the so-called Freedom of Choice Act! And today we say 'no' to . . . late-term abortions right here in our own backyard—abortions so grisly they won't even do them in Europe! We stand up and say 'yes' to life."

I also wanted to make sure that the administrators with UWHC and Meriter Hospital heard our voice, so I quoted the great English apologist C. S. Lewis:

> The greatest evil is not now done in those
> sordid "dens of crime" that Dickens loved to paint.
> It is not done even in concentration camps and
> labour camps. In those we see its final result. The
> greatest evil is conceived and ordered in clean,
> carpeted, warmed, and well-lighted offices, by quiet
> men with white collars and cut fingernails and
> smooth-shaven cheeks who do not need to raise
> their voice.[8]

I used Lewis's words to warn the decision makers in Madison. "If any of those quiet men and women with white collars and polished fingernails who have a vote at Meriter or UWHC are listening, here is my message for you: Choose wisely. If you go forward with these evil plans," I declared, "history will not judge you kindly. You will appear in history books next to all the infamous figures whose atrocities only cause us to shudder in disbelief. My friends, this is *the* human rights issue of our generation."

While I hoped that our show of force in the heart of Madison that blustery January day would be enough to move the hearts of the decision makers at UWHC and Meriter, I knew we might very well be in for a long and difficult fight. Referencing John F. Kennedy's inaugural address, I tried to ready our volunteers for a protracted campaign: "Every age requires decent men and women to rise up and protect life and liberty," I said. "My friends, today that torch is passed to a new generation of civil rights leaders. We must not relent. We must not waver. We must not compromise. Millions depend on us."

A GIANT IN THE LAND

After remarks from Bowman and the slate of state leaders concluded, Dr. Haywood Robinson took the stage. Dr. Robinson was the perfect fit for our rally. Madison prides itself on its open-mindedness, its tolerance, and its diversity. But its celebration of diversity rarely goes more than skin deep. People of every color are welcome in Madison—as long as they don't stray from the prevailing orthodoxy of militant, leftist secularism. The liberals of Madison weren't ready for an African American to stand up, poke fun at President Obama, and urge the city to stand up in defense of pre-born children.

Days before the rally, I told Shawn the community wouldn't know how to handle Dr. Robinson. "Shawn, I know this isn't politically correct to say," I said, stumbling for an appropriate way to discuss race. "But in this town, people are never going to expect an African American man to give a pro-life speech. I think he's really going to make an impact. I hope that's not in poor taste for me to say—"

Shawn cut me off. "Oh, he knows that and he *loves* it."

Dr. Robinson's speech didn't disappoint. He introduced himself as "a sinner saved by grace" and shared the powerful story of his conversion from an abortion provider to a pro-life advocate. He denounced the tragedy of abortion, and he challenged Wisconsin's pro-life community.

> We have a giant in the land. The giant in the land devours 4,000 innocent pre-born children every day in our country. The giant in the land is stealing our legacy that God wants to share with us. The giant in the land is standing in your face right now, preparing to open a late-term abortion facility. He's looking in your eyes, spitting in your face, and daring you to stand up and fight. Madisonians, stand up and fight!
>
> Act like David. You will prevail. Madisonians, do like David did. Pick up your spiritual rocks! Take aim! Slay the giant the same way David slew Goliath. You can do it. You can do it. You can take the giant down.

As the crowd began cheering, Dr. Robinson paused for effect before adding, "And . . . cut his head off!" The crowd laughed, and a voice in the front shouted, "Yes, we can!" lampooning the slogan from President Obama's campaign. Dr. Robinson repeated the line. And then he brought down the house by adding another Obama campaign slogan, "And that's change I can believe in!" The crowd roared.

Dr. Robinson yielded the stage to Shawn, whose keynote address would close the rally. Shawn came well prepared. But as he took the stage, a gust of the frigid north wind scattered his notes across Library Mall. It didn't matter. For the next twenty minutes, Shawn dazzled the pro-life faithful with a beautiful speech, intricately weaving together history, culture, the faith, and the dignity of human life.

Perhaps the gust of wind that scattered Shawn's notes was providential. The part of his speech I found most poignant was entirely spontaneous. He warned the University of Wisconsin health system to scrap its late-term abortion plan, describing a phenomenon he called the "Yeah, but" factor. If the school's affiliated hospital and clinics proceeded with this plan to perform late-term abortions, all of UW's other accomplishments would be tainted. Whatever was achieved in the classroom, in the research laboratory, and on the football field would be nullified by the fact that "Yeah, but you're killing babies."

When Shawn concluded his remarks, it was time to march on the Madison Surgery Center. But first, I had an important announcement to make.

"It turns out we had a few more people show up than we expected today," I said. The crowd, now bigger than ever, laughed joyfully. "So, the police are blocking off the streets, and they'll escort us over to the clinic!" Now the crowd was roaring.

Undoubtedly, I will remember the day for the rest of my life. But amidst a day full of excitement, the moment that impacted me the most didn't necessarily have anything to do with abortion or speeches from honored guests or the police escort. My fondest memory is what happened next.

As our rally attendees lined up behind our squad car escort, students from the St. Paul University Catholic Center led the crowd in singing "Amazing Grace." I knelt down on the stage in front of them to hold the microphone. I started singing, but before long I stopped to watch and to listen and to take it all in. Thousands of voices united in song to praise our Lord. I saw Dr. Robinson—eyes closed, hand stretched toward heaven—belting out the lyrics. I saw one of my parish priests, Fr. David Greenfield—who had a scheduling conflict but rushed into town to catch the end of the rally— also singing along. I saw my pro-life colleagues, members of the clergy, lay people, family, friends, total strangers, long-time activists, first-time protesters, Catholics, Protestants, and Evangelicals praise God with one voice. The love these people had for their God, for defenseless babies, and for one another was tangible.

We needed that giant group hug to prepare us for what happened next. Our march spanned many blocks, and the Madisonians whose Saturday afternoon drives were interrupted by the closed streets were infuriated. Multiple participants reported that the rage in the motorists' eyes was visceral.

That rage was exceeded only by the anger we found on the faces of the pro-abortion demonstrators who were waiting for us in front of the Madison Surgery Center. Representing the Students for Choice, NARAL Pro-Choice Wisconsin, Planned Parenthood, and the International Socialist Organization[9]—the same group my wife marched with in college—this group of a few dozen students and a handful of washed-up 1960s hippy retreads hated us. They hated God. And they seemed to relish the thought of killing babies. In an interview with local media, one of the demonstrators, NARAL Pro-Choice Wisconsin Executive Director Lisa Subeck (who now serves in the Wisconsin State Legislature), actually described the provision of late-term abortions as "exciting."[10]

The signs held by our opposition featured the same dated sloganeering the pro-abortion movement has been recycling for ages. Their chanting was even bolder: "Pray. You'll need it. Your cause will be defeated!"

There was no room for dialogue or discussion with the pro-abortion demonstrators; they simply tried to drown out any dissenting voices, serenading us with cries of "Can we do it? Yes, we can. Free abortion on demand!" The pro-abortion contingent was looking for a confrontation and determined to derail our event, but each of their tactics failed more spectacularly than the last.

First, they failed to note that our rally was being held on Library Mall. That was good news for us. The large crowd stretched the ability of our sound system to carry our message, and a noisy counterprotest would have really created a challenge for our speakers. Instead, the pro-abortion agitators gathered in front of the Madison Surgery Center. As Matt Bowman later pointed out, "The pro-abortion protesters spent an hour and a half yelling down at [the Madison Surgery Center]. So, instead of having them disrupt our speeches . . . the clinic got loudly picketed by [abortion supporters] for three hours, [and] we had an undisrupted rally."

This wasn't the socialists' only tactical mistake. Initially, we planned to march on Park Street, which directly connects Library Mall with the Madison Surgery Center. Due to construction and the size of our crowd, the police made a last-minute decision to take a different route and march to the surgery center from behind. As we made our way toward the clinic, the opposition was marching up Park Street, intending to physically blockade our route. By the time they noticed us coming in the back way, it was too late to impede us. They barely made it back to the surgery center before we got there. As the last of our marchers made their way toward the clinic, sidewalk space was at a premium. The socialists attempted to blockade another sidewalk to prevent our marchers from getting to the clinic. The police responded by closing the street, which allowed pro-lifers to flood the area.

While the pro-abortion contingent tried to provoke an incident, the thousands of pro-lifers marching on the Madison Surgery Center refused to take the bait. Even Madison's self-styled "progressive" newspaper, the *Capital Times,* described our presence as "mostly silent" in the face of "shouted slogans."[11]

Bowman noted that the contrast between the two groups created a major black eye for the abortion proponents, saying, "Meriter and [UWHC] don't care that there are pro-choice nuts who support them. They hate public upheaval from any viewpoint on their street corner."

Amidst the chaos, two images stand out. The first was Amy Hying, who brought 40 Days for Life to Madison. Amy found herself right in the heart of the pro-abortion enclave. The contrast was stunning. The faces around her were contorted by palpable rage, but Amy's bore a radiant smile that exuded the joy and the love of Christ. She stood her ground, silently smiling. She didn't need to utter a word; her peaceful expression spoke volumes.

The second image was of Dr. Robinson walking over to talk with the abortion supporters. Just as I had predicted to Shawn, they took one look at his skin and assumed he was on their side. They weren't expecting him to calmly and articulately make the case for life. And when one of the counterprotesters demonstrated an openness to his message, one of the harder core socialists quickly escorted her away from the discussion.

After we spent the better part of an hour peacefully witnessing in front of the Madison Surgery Center, the police began to clear the streets. Our permit had expired, and it was time to go home. Laura picked Peter up from the babysitter while Amy and I returned Shawn and Dr. Robinson to the airport. Just like that, the event we spent weeks planning was done.

9

Redemption

～～

My parents and brother came to town for the rally, and we met back at our West Side apartment, intending to spend a quiet evening together. But a stream of guests interrupted that quiet evening. First, Amy and her dad dropped in. Then, Will Goodman and his colleague Jen Dunnett from the Servants of Our Lady of Guadalupe arrived. Then Matt Bowman showed up. Before long, our apartment was packed with distinguished pro-lifers who had spent years or even decades serving pre-born children and their mothers as well as some who—scandalized by their beloved university's involvement in a late-term abortion plan—were moved to stand up for life for the first time.

Laura and I frantically started searching for food, grabbing ice cream, frozen pizzas and anything else we could find to entertain our unexpected guests. My parents had intended to spend the evening with us, but with a house full of guests, they decided to head home early.

"No, it's OK," I said. "You are more than welcome to stay for the party."

"That's all right," my mom responded. "This is your night. Celebrate it with your friends."

THE ENIGMATIC PRIEST AND FRIENDS

The funny thing was, except for Amy, Laura and I barely knew any of these folks. I had first met Will and Jen two months ago. Most of the others we had never even met before.

I met, perhaps, the most interesting character of them all earlier that month at our first demonstration outside the Madison Surgery Center when he appeared out of nowhere and listened intently as I conducted an interview with a local television station. As soon as the cameras stopped rolling, he made a beeline to me and corrected one of my statements.

"You said, 'We're here because we *believe* human life begins at conception,'" he told me. "But it's not a belief. It's a scientific fact." The elderly priest drilled his point several times to make sure I grasped it, and then, just as suddenly as he appeared, he was gone. No hello, no goodbye.

I never caught his name and certainly didn't expect to see him again anytime soon. But now here he was, eating pizza and drinking pink lemonade in my living room. Sometime during the course of the evening I learned he was a retired priest who had served as an Army chaplain in Vietnam in the early 1970s. He was also something of an enigma, referring to himself in the third person simply as "the old Army chaplain." And his hurried speech was so rapid that I really had to listen attentively to figure out what he was saying.

The impromptu after-party convened in our living room, and we discussed the day's highs and lows. *How did the day go? How did we feel about the turnout? Where do we go from here? Could the massive backlash in the streets of Madison succeed in derailing UWHC's abortion scheme?* We all agreed the day was an unmitigated success, that the turnout surpassed expectations, and that we needed to keep the pressure on. Most importantly, we held onto hope that maybe, just maybe, the university health system would drop its plan to perform late-term abortions in response to the public outcry.

As the evening went on, members of the group that spontaneously assembled in our little apartment started sharing war stories from pro-life activism of years past. Most of the crew had worked together on the University of Wisconsin campus back in the 1990s through an organization they called the C.A.L.L. (Collegians Activated to Liberate Life) Team. Matt went off to law school and continued his pro-life work with the ADF. At the invitation of then-bishop, now-Cardinal Raymond Burke, Will helped organize the Servants of Our Lady of Guadalupe. And Amy launched 40 Days for Life in Madison.

Each of them had made heroic sacrifices to defend life for years or even decades. What impressed me most was how each had resisted the temptation to despair in the face of the sorrow and the emptiness of the culture. They were joyful warriors, and their pro-life efforts were infused with Christian hope. This was exemplified best by Will, who relayed a hilarious story he called "Sad Mickey."

Back in the late 1990s, the Walt Disney Company hosted a parade in Wisconsin. Dismayed by some of the family-unfriendly content the entertainment giant distributed, Will and some friends registered for a pro-life, pro-family entry in the parade. The city tried to oppose their inclusion in the parade, but it was a public event. Attorneys got involved, and ultimately the pro-life, pro-family presence in the parade was secured. The entry created quite the scene: a truck, balloons, and clowns handing out information explaining Disney's anti-family productions, support for sexual deviancy, use of child labor, and other offenses. The highlight of the exhibit, however, was a volunteer dressed up as Mickey Mouse—made up with a big frowning face. Disney tried to divert attention from Sad Mickey and even encouraged spectators in the stands to boo. It was a sight to behold, and Will's retelling of it brought down the house. The stories from throughout the years continued as we sat and talked and celebrated and laughed deep into the night.

GOD'S NOT DONE WITH US YET

Alongside family occasions like births, sacraments, and my wedding, the day stands among the best of my life. After spending the evening celebrating with friends, I couldn't help but to reflect on a moment from earlier that day. As we prepared for the rally, I caught a glimpse of my boss from my previous job as she walked through Library Mall. Only a few months earlier, she had relieved me of my duties as a technical writer, plunging me into one of the most difficult periods of my life.

The loss of my employment was particularly painful because I hadn't really enjoyed success at the job I held before that either. Right out of college, I turned down an intriguing position as a writer—a job I was well suited for and would have loved—to accept an opportunity in the fund-raising and donor development office at a prestigious Chicago-area university. It didn't take long to realize I had made the wrong decision.

One of my responsibilities involved helping to host a screening for a film promoting embryonic stem cell research being done at the university. I knew this research involved destroying and experimenting on human beings, and it troubled me a great deal. At the same time, I worried that refusing the assignment would cost me my job. Torn about what to do, I sought the advice of friends and family members, who advised me to carry on with my work. "The research will continue whether or not you assist with the film," they said. "You're not responsible for it." The advice seemed dubious, but I lacked the moral courage to investigate further. I had received the answer I wanted, and I took the path of least resistance—one of the greatest regrets of my life. Thank God for confession.

Within a year, it became clear the office was in transition, and, over the course of eighteen months, more than half of the staff turned over. A number of my former colleagues did not leave by choice. I saw where things were headed and left on my own terms. We moved to Wisconsin.

To some extent, circumstances beyond my control were to blame for my failing career, but I hadn't made the most of the opportunity. Only two years into my marriage, I couldn't help but to think that I had a wife and a young child depending on me to earn a living for them, and I had already failed at two different jobs. Questions swirled around me. How would I support my family? Did my in-laws feel that their daughter had married a loser? Would I find a way to pick up the pieces? And if so, how long would it take?

The fall of 2008 was something like a George Bailey moment for me. Like the iconic character from *It's a Wonderful Life*, I had hit rock bottom. Yes, my family was supportive. But in my darker moments—and there were a lot of them—I found myself on the brink of despair, wondering whether my failings would ruin the lives of my wife and son. The previous six months had been incredibly difficult.

But tonight was different. Tonight, state and national pro-life leaders were gathered in my home to celebrate that we had helped organize the largest pro-life event in the state in recent memory.

Perhaps God wasn't done with me yet.

Others could see our newfound hope too. Days later, I was talking with my mom by phone. She could tell something was wrong. In fact, Laura and I had just had an argument, and I was upset about it. Mom knew exactly what to say.

"That's too bad. If you're angry, I hope you can think back to the rally on Saturday. I saw the love in your eyes as you two looked at each other from across the stage," she said. "I hope you can work things out quickly because it would be sad to let a disagreement spoil that."

"Gosh, Mom, it's hard to stay mad when you put it that way."

As the week continued, speculation mounted. With thousands of people packing the streets of Madison, would our rally be enough to deter the University of Wisconsin health system and Meriter Hospital from shedding the blood of innocent, nearly viable children?

We didn't know. But like William Wilberforce and the band of relentless abolitionists that inspired me in *Amazing Grace*, we were resolved to keep up the fight as long as we needed to.

10

We Begin to Fight

~~~

With an assist from the antics of the pro-abortion agitators, our rally dominated the local news cycle and even made some national headlines. And because it was held over the weekend, that buzz stretched from Saturday all the way into the workweek.

For the most part, the coverage was decent, but I was disappointed in the numbers local newspapers put out. One Christian website claimed 5,000 people marched with us. I knew that number was high, but the *Capital Times* reported that only 800 people attended.[1] We knew that number was way off—albeit not as wrong as one student publication that claimed "dozens" of pro-lifers joined the event. (Technically, though, I suppose that's true. *Hundreds of dozens* of pro-lifers braved the elements to stand for life.) Our best estimates indicated 2,000 to 2,500 people marched with us.

Meriter's board of directors had already approved the late-term abortion plan, a fact that grieved me all the more upon finding out that another Wisconsin Badger— football hero and former Athletic Director Pat Richter—

was a member of that board.[2] All eyes now focused on the UWHC board, which was scheduled to meet and vote on the plan on Wednesday, February 4.

We had no idea what outcome to expect. In the final message to Vigil for Life supporters before the vote, I wrote, "My friends, I don't know what our chances of winning tomorrow are. But win or lose, know that our efforts have not been in vain. We have stood to defend truth and innocence in a world gone mad."

THE FIX IS IN

In the lead-up to the UWHC vote, board members and administrators received thousands of phone calls and emails from both sides of the debate. Some of their lines were even rerouted because of the sheer volume of calls as UWHC set up a line where concerned citizens could leave a voice mail to weigh in.

Our efforts to rally pro-lifers to speak out made an impact. The 2,836 calls and emails opposing the abortion scheme more than doubled those in support. Those calls and emails were in addition to the many directed toward individual staff and board members. The number of letters to board members opposing the plan more than quadrupled the number of letters in support.

Because of the controversy, the meeting was packed with both supporters and opponents of the abortion plan. Activists, lobbyists, medical professionals, and regular citizens—some of them getting involved in the abortion debate for the first time—converged upon the meeting site in nearby Middleton. I had to park at a Costco close to the meeting and was surprised to see a heavy police presence as I walked the rest of the way. Just to enter the meeting space, we needed to pass through a police checkpoint.[3]

We'd later learn that we weren't being monitored by the local police department only. Prior to the UWHC board meeting, the Department of Homeland Security (DHS) violated its own guidelines by conducting a threat assessment investigation aimed at leaders on both sides of the controversy. The investigation made national news when it was made public amidst a lawsuit by a government watchdog group called the Electronic Frontier Foundation.[4]

On one hand, a DHS memo claimed the bogus investigation most likely wouldn't "have any impact on civil liberties or civil rights."[5] On the other hand, when pro-lifers requested a copy of the report via open-records request, Middleton Police Capt. Noel Kakuske refused to provide the document, writing, "Disclosure would result in the identification and public disclosure of individuals affiliated with groups on both sides of the issue, which would place them in danger from opposing radical extremists."[6]

Kakuske's refusal to provide the report was odd. DHS claimed to have destroyed its copies of the report. So why didn't the Middleton Police Department do the same? Secondly, none of the leaders from either side appeared to be concerned about concealing their identities. Our names had been disseminated widely by mainstream media outlets, event promotions, and email lists. And finally, given that no less an authority than DHS had determined the individuals investigated posed no security threat, what "radical extremists" was Kakuske so worried about?

Answers to these questions never came. Through a series of strategic legal requests, a number of my fellow pro-life leaders and I were able to confirm that we were, indeed, targets of the investigation. Amidst a heavily redacted section of the report, my entry simply stated that I had no known law enforcement contacts. The revelation that DHS violated its own intelligence-gathering guidelines led the department to destroy the report, to provide "remedial training" to the analyst who prepared it, and to send federal attorneys to counsel the analyst's supervisors.[7] Again, all to find out that my friends and I had no history of legal trouble.

In any case, the meeting took place amidst a circus-like atmosphere. A few pro-lifers came to protest or to pray outside the building. One family from St. Louis even drove more than five hours up to Madison just to stand in front of the building and pray. They came filled with conviction but without a plan, and we ended up hosting them overnight in our tiny apartment after learning they needed accommodations.

But most people wanted to sit in on the meeting. The room quickly filled to capacity, and many attendees were forced to view the proceedings on closed-circuit television from an overflow room. Even Dr. Bill Evans was denied entry, even though he was the clear leader of the pro-life medical community's opposition to the abortion scheme. So much for an open meeting.

The meeting began with a presentation from Dr. Laurel Rice, Department of Obstetrics and Gynecology chairperson and a professor in the Division of Gynecology Oncology at the University of Wisconsin-Madison School of Medicine and Public Health. Rice, an abortion provider herself, argued that the Madison Surgery Center was the proper location for abortions up to twenty-two weeks of gestation because no other health-care providers had stepped up in the wake of the supposed retirement of late-term abortionist Dennis

Christiansen. The Madison Surgery Center, Rice said, was a proper fit as it was "close to a surgical suite and blood bank [because] there is a higher complication rate [for late-term abortions]."

The myth of Christiansen's retirement wasn't the only statement of questionable veracity Rice made. She also insisted, "There's no research [of tissue harvested from aborted babies] associated with this proposal." While there was no way to prove her claim false, pro-lifers later took notice of a 2014 study that thanked Caryn Dutton, the late-term abortion plan architect, for her "support with tissue collection."[8]

Rice chillingly ended her presentation proclaiming the availability of second-trimester abortions at the Madison Surgery Center is "what I want for my sister, my daughter, my mother, any family member and all friends."

Fielding questions from the UWHC board, Rice also admitted that 75 percent of the late-term abortions at the Madison Surgery Center would be elective—that is, not motivated by any health considerations. She also revealed that abortion training would be part of standard training for medical school residents.

Following Rice's presentation, UWHC invited testimony from several organizations supporting the abortion plan and several groups opposing it. Each group was given the same amount of time to make its case, and board members were permitted to ask questions following the testimony.

The pro-life groups invited included Pro-Life Wisconsin and Wisconsin Right to Life. The testimonies were rational, balancing a well-articulated concern for the rights of pre-born children under the natural moral law with a warning about some of the more practical consequences UWHC would face should it proceed with its plan. Pro-life advocates described the humanity of the pre-born child, highlighting milestones of fetal development and capacity for pain. And they illustrated the regret and emotional health toll that abortion takes on women.

No fair-minded observer could have concluded that the pro-life case was based on some sort of superstitious, religious fanaticism. Each of the pro-life speakers provided opposition that was clear, grounded, and reasonable. Initially, I thought this boded well for our position. For nearly a month, pro-lifers had demonstrated mass support, combining sixty thousand signed petitions with boots on the ground the previous weekend. And now the masses were being reinforced by dispassionate testimony from our movement's leaders.

In reality, that dispassionate testimony was no match for the political skills of pro-abortion representatives at the meeting. Planned Parenthood and its allies didn't have a compelling rational argument in favor of performing late-term abortions at the Madison Surgery Center. There wasn't one. Instead, they wove together a tapestry of emotional arguments, circular logic, and outright absurdities.

Planned Parenthood Public Policy Director Chris Taylor (now a state judge) insisted that the lack of access to abortion is indisputably linked to negative maternal health outcomes. She asserted that the "highest maternal mortality rates" are found in "war-torn" countries that "have no abortion care." Specifically, Taylor referenced Afghanistan and Somalia as countries where "maternal health suffers." Of course, any reasonable person would recognize that women in these countries suffer because they are "war-torn" rather than due to a lack of abortion.

Perhaps Taylor, too, understood, but sometimes facts get in the way of the narrative. After all, from earthquakes to floods to famine, Planned Parenthood's response to every natural disaster or humanitarian crisis is to export birth control and abortion.

The abortion lobby didn't—and couldn't—answer the big questions about when life begins, about the intrinsic value of human life, about the natural law, and about whether the lives of people who suffer have value. So, abortion proponents didn't even try. Instead, they pulled at the heartstrings with anecdotes aimed at framing support for late-term abortion as compassionate. And in doing so, they made the more measured rhetoric of the pro-life speakers appear cold and aloof. And whereas the pro-life speakers came representing their particular organizations, one radio host privately suggested to me that the pro-abortion groups coordinated their efforts. The result was a dazzling display of political savvy that we, frankly, were no match for.

For the first time, our optimism began to wane. We found no encouragement from the response of the board members either. While each speaker was allotted a limited amount of time to speak, there was no such restriction on the question-and-answer session. While few questions were asked of the pro-life speakers, the board repeatedly lobbed up softballs to the abortion supporters, significantly extending their time at the microphone.

The fix was in.

The board briefly adjourned before reconvening to discuss the issue themselves and make a decision. Two board members thanked the attendees for their concern and passion regardless of which side they took on the matter. A few board members raised vague concerns with the plan.

Then pleasantries and frivolities were set aside as one board member began a monologue:

> We've heard a lot about "Life begins at con-
> ception," and "Abortion is taking a life. All life is
> sacred, and we must protect the unborn."
> There's disappointment about a highly
> respected institution that spends a lot of time
> saving lives that would be involved in something
> that, in the perspective of the speaker, takes a life.
> . . . and those are classic arguments about abor-
> tion. In my world, being a lawyer, I tend to try to
> be more black-and-white, and I would suggest the
> problem with those arguments . . . is the beginning
> assumption of when life begins.
> And when we talk about taking a life, we
> assume that that is a life. Yet we have a decision by
> the United States Supreme Court that says that the
> viability isn't there and that it's not life, but that,
> more important than anything, women have a right
> to control their bodies. And government . . . don't
> [sic] have a right to say anything about that.
> The burden for me was "how do you take that
> constitutional right and deprive them of it by
> denying them a comprehensive medical service, and
> specifically this service? . . . I feel that we have to
> go ahead and approve this because I think we have
> that responsibility and can't be part of a conspiracy
> to deny a constitutional right. . . . The politics and
> what price you pay and the economics? . . . I'm
> willing to take that risk."

The statement was an astonishing blend of ignorance and arrogance. The *Roe v. Wade* decision never held that "it's not a life." In fact, writing for the majority, Justice Harry Blackmun sidestepped the question entirely stating, "We need not resolve the difficult question of when life begins. . . . [The Court] at this point in the development of man's knowledge, is not in position to speculate as to the answer."[9] Blackmun's copout was utter nonsense at the time. Experts in genetics and embryology had long known that life begins at conception. And if Blackmun's ignorance as to when life begins was absurd in 1973, it was even more absurd nearly four decades later when technological developments like 4D ultrasound provide a window to the womb, illustrating the clear humanity of the pre-born child.

But the UWHC Authority Board wasn't interested. Its callous indifference toward the violent taking of human life was shocking in its banality.

That evening, the board learned all about the humanity of pre-born children. A doctor described why abortion isn't needed to save a mother's life. Board members learned that pre-born children are capable of feeling pain. They heard about the physical risks of abortion. They had been instructed about the emotional trauma caused by abortion.

The board had received thousands of pieces of correspondence from Wisconsin citizens opposing the late-term abortion plan and was aware of tens of thousands of petitions denouncing the plan. Board members knew of thousands more marching in the streets, even receiving a police escort to close down those streets. They were told of staff opposition, the threat of lawsuits, and possible fiscal ruin for the Madison Surgery Center.

But the UWHC Authority Board didn't care. All of these concerns amounted to—as the pontificating board member put it—"a risk I'm willing to take." He might as well have asked, "What is Truth?"

As the board members prepared to vote, I felt like a defendant on trial for a capital crime as the jury enters the courtroom. Only, it wasn't my life on the line but the lives of hundreds of defenseless children. A voice vote was taken. Eleven members of the board voted to approve the late-term abortion plan. Three voted to oppose.

"It was a low point for all of us," Dr. Nancy Fredericks, the courageous pro-life doctor who first sounded the alarm so many months ago, later said.[10]

BEGINNING TO FIGHT

The evening was getting late, so a couple dozen pro-lifers met at a local restaurant for dinner. We remained joyful on the outside, confident that we had given it our best. But deep down, we were heartbroken.

Heading home that night, my phone rang. The number wasn't familiar. The hurried voice on the other end of the line most assuredly was.

"It's the old Army chaplain."

"How are you doing?" I asked as I pondered just how in the world he'd gotten my phone number.

"How'd it go tonight?" he asked.

"Well, we lost," I muttered, filled with bitterness and more than a little self-pity.

The chaplain's sharp rebuke once again caught me by surprise.

"Of course, you lost!" he told me. "You haven't been at this pro-life work very long, have you? This is when we *begin* to fight!"

And so, we did.

The Madison Surgery Center board met Friday, February 6 for a vote to finalize the abortion plan. With UWHC, UW Medical Foundation, and Meriter having already approved the plan, this vote was a mere formality, and the plan passed unanimously, 6-0.[11]

After the plan was approved, I received a call from a local reporter asking to interview me for my response on behalf of Vigil for Life. Living with a toddler and having spent the previous month running our campaign against the Madison Surgery Center's abortion scheme out of my living room, my home was much too messy to clean up in time for an afternoon interview. Fortunately, the reporter agreed to meet me in our apartment complex's parking lot.

Though I can't remember his exact words, the reporter asked me something to the effect of, "Well, you lost the vote. What are you going to do now?"

The chaplain's admonition the night before was still fresh in my mind as I responded.

"We're not going anywhere," I said defiantly. "We're going to continue to show up and pray in front of that building until this plan is canceled once and for all."

As the words came out of my mouth, I wondered whether I might be writing a check I wouldn't be able to cash. What was I committing myself to? The UWHC board demonstrated that it wouldn't be deterred even by thousands of people stopping traffic on campus, sixty thousand petitions from the public, and a mounting boycott from both its patients and the medical community. I might be pledging to pray in front of that building for years—or even decades!

So be it. I had made a promise, and—come what may—I intended to keep it. Even if it was only me praying at the Madison Surgery Center, it was a fight that needed to be fought, regardless of the long odds against us. Even if we had no chance at all of victory, continuing to witness in defense of the lives of the children who would be lost was the right thing to do.

11

To Save a Mockingbird

~~~

The roots of the resilience I pledged to the reporter in the parking lot of my apartment stretch back to my childhood. Growing up, reading was an important part of my day-to-day life. My mother taught me to read as a kindergartner, well before I had the chance to learn in school. She taped home-made flashcards bearing the spelling of common household items throughout our house to help us begin to recognize the correlation among letters, sounds, and words. The method of instruction was easy for anyone to understand, with the possible exception of a distant relative who, upon visiting, observed one of the cards and inquired, "Cup-board? What is a cup-board?"

Mom frequently read aloud to my brother Brad and me, progressing through the "Dick and Jane" series to children's chapter books. Family time with a book was so well established in our home that we'd continue to read aloud together well after my brother and I became comfortable with the written word. Eventually, we moved on to novels.

While I continue to cherish the memory of curling up on the couch with my mom and my brother a quarter century later, I'll confess I've forgotten the title of every book we shared—except for one.

"What's it about?" I asked my mother when she suggested we tackle Harper Lee's classic *To Kill a Mockingbird*. After all, the title is more than a little curious to a grade school student. I didn't find her response particulárly compelling, but Mom thought it was a great book, so that was good enough for me. It didn't take more than a few chapters for me to fall in love with it.

If you haven't read it, the book chronicles the plight of an attorney deep in the Jim Crow South as he raises his two children following the death of their mother. That task becomes significantly more difficult for Atticus Finch when he agrees to defend Tom Robinson, a black man falsely accused of rape. Robinson is a good and virtuous man, clearly innocent of the charges leveled against him by the trashiest family in town. But old prejudices don't disappear easily, and for most of the town, the color of a man's skin is all the evidence needed to determine guilt. As a result, Robinson finds himself fighting for his life.

Atticus, meanwhile, finds himself in for the fight of *his* life. He's a strong enough figure to endure being hated for defending a black man. The greater challenge is defending and protecting his children, who inherit the scorn of the community as well.

Every summary or book review I've ever read of *To Kill a Mockingbird* describes it as a book about the struggle against racism in the Jim Crow–era South. And that's certainly true. But I've long felt that these reviews (as well as the critically acclaimed movie) miss the heart of the book: it's a story about growing up. Told from the perspective of Atticus's eight-year-old daughter Scout, it's a book about the pain and the loss of innocence that occur when a child encounters real injustice for the very first time. It's a story about learning to do what's right, even when it hurts.

I'm not sure how many times I've re-read *To Kill a Mockingbird* since I first encountered it with my family in the living room of the house where I grew up. I'd guess at least a half-dozen times. And every time, I'm blessed with a different point of view. As a nine-year-old, I read the book through Scout's eyes. In adolescence, I grasped the vantage point of her older brother Jem: moody, sullen, and more than a bit self-righteous. As I neared adulthood, I found myself moved by Atticus's perspective. Now a grown man with young children of my own, I've come full-circle, reading the words of young Scout with a renewed appreciation for life through the eyes of a child.

As our campaign against the university health system's late-term abortion plan reached its darkest hour, one line from the book particularly moved me. Atticus, Scout, and Jem have met their darkest hour. The backlash against the Finch family has reached a crescendo. Townsfolk, neighbors, and even family members are making sport of heaping verbal abuse on the children in retaliation for their father's spirited defense of a black man.

In the face of intense persecution, Atticus tells his children, "I wanted you to see what real courage is . . . It's when you know you're licked before you begin, but you begin anyway and see it through no matter what. You rarely win, but sometimes you do."[1]

This line hit home. As pro-lifers, we were licked. The Madison Surgery Center had already begun hiring additional staff, and the instruments that would be used to perform the abortions had been delivered.[2] But we weren't about to go down without a fight. We began anyway, vowing to see it through no matter what.

BLOWING OFF STEAM

After the Madison Surgery Center officially approved its plan to perform late-term abortions, our breakneck pace subsided. From Matt Bowman's call to the demonstration a couple days later, the press conference, the petitions, the calls, and the rally on Library Mall, the previous six weeks had been a steady build toward the UWHC vote. Now, it was over. We expected abortions to begin within a few weeks, and surely that would launch another flurry of activity. But, at the moment, things were eerily quiet. We remained committed to keeping the pressure on the UW health system, but I wasn't quite sure what to do next.

That's when I learned that ESPN would be coming to Madison to host its Saturday morning college basketball pre-game show on Valentine's Day. The Wisconsin Men's Basketball program was riding high. Two years earlier, it achieved its first-ever number-one ranking and was now a perennial participant in March Madness. A visit from the ESPN *College GameDay* crew would showcase the university to the nation. Fans were invited to attend the live broadcast and to bring a heavy dose of school spirit as the cameras panned the crowd going into and coming out of commercial breaks.

This was an opportunity. This was a chance to capitalize on Shawn's "Yeah, but…" principle.

"The basketball team at the University of Wisconsin is dominating the competition!"

"Yeah, but the university hospital is killing babies."

I decided I'd attend the pre-game show, and I'd bring a sign condemning UWHC's abortion plan with me.

We had suspected that UW Health administrators believed they could simply wait out the immediate backlash and that the controversy would fade just as quickly as it erupted. I wanted to send them a message that we were in this long-term—that as long as lives were being lost, we'd be a thorn in their side. Though the school might accomplish a great many things, we would stick around as its conscience, reminding students, parents, faculty, administration, and donors that there was something dramatically wrong on campus.

One of our volunteers named Jeanne Breunig always seemed to have a new pro-life sign at our vigils. I asked for her assistance. She delivered, working with a local sign-making company to equip me for Valentine's Day at the basketball arena.

The result was a masterpiece: a two-part sign. The first part displayed a message celebrating the Badger basketball team. The second sign implored the university health system to drop its abortion plan. Using Velcro, we stuck the signs together and sealed off the edges with tape to obscure the gap between them, concealing the pro-life message.

My sign-hidden-within-a-sign in tow, I arrived at the Kohl Center early on Valentine's Day, hoping to get a good spot to make an appearance on national television. I didn't arrive quite early enough, and a sizable crowd had already assembled. As I waited in line for the doors to open, security staff inspected my sign no fewer than five times. Fortunately, Jeanne's work with the Velcro and tape was stellar. The sign was approved at each checkpoint.

I found my seat and waited for the show to begin. In the minutes before we went on air, ESPN's on-air talent took the stage. Many of the commentators—Dick Vitale, Digger Phelps, and former coach Bobby Knight—were college basketball legends. Meanwhile, ESPN staff prepared the crowd for its national close-up, instructing the crowd when exactly to go nuts for the hometown Badgers. The overhead camera panned the crowd, and Wisconsin fans erupted just as they had been coached.

Now that I was in the stadium, I was nervous. When would be the best time to display the sign? I wasn't sure. I waited and waited, trying to work up the courage. Finally, about twenty minutes into the broadcast, I decided it was now or never. I took my keys out of my pocket and used them to saw away at the tape. It must have been quite a bizarre sight. After all, I already looked a bit out of place showing up alone. The fans next to me must have been beyond curious when I started hacking away at my sign.

When *College GameDay* resumed following a commercial break, I raised my pro-life sign. Every time the cameras cut to the crowd, I held it as high as I could. Arena staff saw it immediately. When ESPN cut away for another commercial break, security officers made a beeline for me.

"You need to give us the sign."

"I'll just leave," I responded. "I'm here to hold the sign, not to watch basketball."

The officer clearly didn't know what to make of it. I wasn't there to give him a hard time, though. I was there to make a statement. I had made it, and rather than make a scene, I stood up and shuffled my way toward the aisle to let him escort me out. As I walked up the steps toward the exit, I held my sign high for all to see.

"Put the sign down, sir," the security guard ordered.

I ignored him, defiantly raising the sign my entire way out of the arena. As I did, a chorus of boos serenaded me. "This isn't a political event!" one clearly disgusted spectator shouted. "It's basketball!"

I suppose you could say this was my "Sad Mickey" moment. After six weeks of frustration, I'll admit it felt pretty good to blow off some steam at the expense of my alma mater. But as much fun as it was to get jeered out of the stadium where I spent my college days cheering, it was time to get back to work. Abortions were due to begin at the Madison Surgery Center as soon as the end of the month.

GROWING BACKLASH

Though the board voted to approve the late-term abortion plan, it became clear that public backlash was quickly taking a toll on the entire university health system as Madison Surgery Center patients began canceling appointments. Staff members were caught off guard and struggled to handle the wave of canceled appointments.[3] Even many "pro-choice" patients opposed the provision of late-term abortions that were entirely elective.[4]

Wisconsin Right to Life helped maximize the boycott's impact with a newspaper ad reading, "Patients . . . It's time to say 'No!' to medical treatment at the Madison Surgery Center where late-term abortions are planned. . . . Time to say NO to your medical care payments helping to subsidize late-term abortions. Time to tell your doctor to treat you somewhere else."[5]

One of our Vigil for Life volunteers wasn't quite ready to change health-care providers, but that changed when she arrived for her first prenatal visit at a UW clinic. "I told [the nurse] I was uncomfortable with the potential of working with the OB involved in doing abortions at Planned Parenthood and attempting to start them at the Madison Surgery Center," Alissa Hirscher wrote in a letter to the editor of the *Wisconsin State Journal*. "I explained the contradiction I saw in delivering babies for some families and taking them from others. I was told, 'But it would be fine for you, because you want your baby, don't you?' I voiced my objection to thinking that babies gained value on whether they were wanted or not.'"

That led Alissa to find a new doctor. "I left my appointment shaken and upset, and immediately canceled future appointments. UW lost my business—nine months of prenatal care, a delivery and follow-ups—because of their casual and inconsistent view of life. I am another patient taking the care of me and my baby elsewhere."[6]

One of our volunteers even shared with us an email he sent, withdrawing from a University of Wisconsin sleep study he was participating in.

The rebellion wasn't limited to patients. Doctors and entire physician groups ceased referring patients to the Madison Surgery Center for care.[7] A pediatric specialist from one of Wisconsin's most esteemed health-care systems summarized the collective mood of the state's medical community in an email to Meriter CEO Jim Woodward, writing:

It is beyond troubling that a network of a
highly revered hospital and clinics would decide to
get into the business of late-term abortion. Effective immediately, I will not refer any more patients
to your institutions. Having discussed this matter
with numerous colleagues (as well as citizens
throughout the state), it is clear that the majority of
the public stands with me. Should you proceed with
this venture, there will be ramifications that span
the state. I adamantly suggest you reconsider provision of abortions at the Madison Surgery Center.

The effects of the boycott were visible to patients as well.
Vigil for Life volunteers reported that, when they needed
medical care, they were told they would have to wait weeks
to be seen across town. But, if they wanted to go to the Madison Surgery Center, they could get an appointment within
days.

"People were calling their insurance companies and
saying, 'Unless you can get me into some kind of a health
care facility that is not associated with the UW, I am going
to change my insurance policy,'" said Wisconsin Family
Network Director Julaine Appling. "There were people calling and boycotting MSC like crazy. And the impact on the
bottom line was tremendous."[8]

The entire pro-life world, it seemed, was souring on the
state's beloved university. Laura and I were no longer proud
of our identity as alumni. Over time, we just quit following Badger football, basketball, and hockey. It's not that
I started to actively root against the school I used to love; I
just couldn't bring myself to celebrate an institution so thoroughly invested in the destruction of innocent human life.

Eventually, the Wisconsin flag, autographed Badger basketball pennant, and even our diplomas made their way to a cardboard box in our apartment's storage unit. We were done.

Meanwhile, the Madison Surgery Center staff was in open revolt. Even medical personnel who weren't necessarily pro-life were unhappy that they were not informed about the abortion plan earlier, and more employees joined Dr. Nancy Fredericks in working with Matt Bowman, who assisted in drafting legal letters and conscience statements.[9]

Executives from the three entities that owned the Madison Surgery Center were forced to scramble. The drop in patients followed the 2008 recession, leading UW Medical Foundation President and CEO Jeff Grossman to write to his colleagues, "We need to track cancellations as accurately as possible...When all this began I told Laurel [Rice, co-architect of the plan] and Caryn [Dutton, the abortion provider] that we could not put our whole operation at economic risk to achieve their goals."[10]

By mid-February, UW Health administrators sent staff members an email providing instructions on damage control. "We understand that some of you are receiving calls or patient comments in clinic as a result of the Madison Surgery Center decision to offer second-trimester pregnancy termination services," the email read. "We would like to provide the following guidelines for handling these interactions as well as any email or written correspondence you receive on this topic."[11]

The message included a fact sheet that health-care providers and support staff could use to deflect criticism. The document's very first line made it clear that the fact sheet was thinly veiled propaganda: "The decision to terminate a pregnancy is an intensely personal one, permitted by the laws of Wisconsin and the United States government."[12] That wasn't entirely true. Interestingly, abortion is largely illegal under a Wisconsin law still on the books.[13] The state is simply prohibited from enforcing the law by order of the United States Supreme Court.[14]

The email also included a script "to ensure that we are giving a consistent message throughout the organization." This script directed UW Health employees to "try not to engage in specifics" but to instead funnel feedback to a single public relations email address and phone number.[15] The goal was to insulate staff from opposition to the abortion plans, making patient feedback easier to ignore.

Just as Grossman's letter suggested, the email did ask staff to track the number of calls they received from patients canceling appointments due to the abortion plans. Clearly, UW Health was concerned about the financial ramifications of its decision. In response, pro-life groups around the state ramped up the financial pressure by circulating a letter that Madison Surgery Center patients could use to inform their health-care providers that they did not want to receive treatment in the same facility where abortions were being performed on twenty-week-old unborn babies. This, we believed, was key. You didn't have to be a committed pro-lifer to be squeamish about the idea of visiting your doctor in one room while a five-month-old unborn baby was being dismembered in the next.

While the administration tried to insulate staff from feedback, we argued that patients had a right to share their concerns directly with their health-care providers rather than being redirected to a generic hotline. We worked to ensure the dialogue continued with the medical community, not with the public relations professionals. Patients were urged to tell doctors and nurses, "I know you have a UW public affairs script—please listen to me instead of reading your script."

In March, Pro-Life Wisconsin held its biennial Day at the Capitol, where pro-lifers from around the state come to learn how to effectively engage their legislators. Top pro-life lawmakers address the audience, and, after the workshop ends, participants head to the offices of their local representatives. With the Madison Surgery Center still a hot topic, Matt Sande invited me to give a half-hour-long speech with an update.

I provided the attendees with the background story of the late-term abortion plan, starting with that first surprising phone call from Matt Bowman. I shared how the resistance grew behind the scenes. And I reflected, once again, on the little girl with Down syndrome, whose beautiful smile moved me to redouble our efforts to derail the Madison Surgery Center's abortion plan.

I particularly noted that while the UW officials had waffled on their motives for getting into the late-term abortion business, they never wavered from the fact that they want to provide a place to "terminate" babies with abnormalities. They were looking to sign a large-scale death warrant for children with disabilities.

I couldn't help but to be reminded of the point in *To Kill a Mockingbird* when Miss Maudie explains the book's title. She says, "Mockingbirds don't do one thing but make music for us to enjoy. They don't eat up people's gardens, don't nest in corncribs, they don't do one thing but sing their hearts out for us. That's why it's a sin to kill a mockingbird."[16]

"Special needs kids like [those targeted by UWHC] don't do one thing but smile their hearts out for us," I said.

"And that's why it's a sin to kill them. Yet that's exactly what the UW and Meriter intend to do. It's a world gone mad."

Pro-Life Wisconsin launched a new website to serve as an online clearinghouse for Wisconsinites looking to keep the pressure on the university health system. It also ramped up a series of television ads on the local network affiliates, further driving public opinion against UWHC's decision. While television advertising is expensive, state residents were upset, and the money came in easily.

We were also pleased to see Madison's Catholic hospital, St. Mary's, launch an advertising campaign highlighting its childbirth program. I don't know whether the St. Mary's decision to place billboards of adorable babies all over town was deliberately timed to provide contrast with the other two Madison hospitals' participation in grisly late-term abortions. From our perspective, however, the juxtaposition could not have been more perfect.

Meanwhile, Vigil for Life needed to determine how to proceed. My heart sank as I considered what it would feel like to learn that the first human life had ended at the hospital my alma mater runs. I knew I'd be upset—perhaps too upset to compose a message to our faithful prayer warriors who had given their all to prevent the loss of life. I recalled the story about how Gen. Dwight D. Eisenhower prepared two addresses for American troops following the D-Day invasion of northern France in June 1944. One reported victory. The other came to be known as the "In Case of Failure Letter" that would be read in the event of a defeat.[17] I prepared for the worst, drafting a letter in advance that I could send out by email after the first abortion day.

We considered participating in our first ever spring 40 Days for Life campaign. The 40 Days for Life headquarters offers the opportunity to lead campaigns in both the spring and the fall. In Madison, our fall campaign has always taken every last bit of energy we have. We stand in uninterrupted vigil for forty straight days and wear ourselves out. Certainly, we stayed active in between campaigns, but we had never taken on the spring campaign.

While the idea of a campaign near campus was enticing, we ultimately felt we didn't have the manpower to pull it off, especially on short notice. Instead, we began rallying volunteers to pray and witness when they were able to. My heart always swelled with pride in our participants as I drove through town and happened to see them praying in front of the building.

While we weren't yet ready to host a forty-day vigil, we decided we'd host a forty-hour vigil during Holy Week. And this time, instead of going to the Madison Surgery Center, we'd take our presence to the belly of the beast. We set up shop in front of the University of Wisconsin Hospital itself. Another volunteer and I launched the vigil at 8:00 p.m. on Wednesday. From that hour through noon on Good Friday, we had at least two volunteers on the sidewalk in front of the hospital praying and holding signs.

The hospital itself was on the opposite side of campus, and we wanted to make sure UWHC officials weren't insulated from the pro-life backlash. Furthermore, setting up in front of the headquarters would reach another audience. UW Health features a nationally renowned children's hospital. How could the health system work so hard to save the lives of kids on one side of campus and then dismember them on the other side? How would hospital patients feel about UW doctors ending lives, while they fought for their own lives? We weren't necessarily targeting any particular demographic, but we did want to create a public relations problem. A member of the UW faculty later confirmed to us that our presence infuriated UW Health officials.

We continued striving to undermine the abortion scheme any way possible, emailing medical school faculty members to politely explain our concerns about the abortion plan. We didn't receive a response, but our goal was to make sure that the university would not be able to tuck its abortion plan neatly into the margins. Meanwhile, the Madison Surgery Center itself was located right by the Kohl Center, so we protested and handed out literature in front of the building prior to Badger hockey games.

Backlash to the university health system's abortion plan would be no passing storm. Shawn Carney's "Yeah, but" principle was here to stay.

12

In It for the Long Haul

~~~

While UW Health said abortions would start within weeks, we were relieved as weeks turned into months, and still no abortions had been performed. Clearly, the ADF's warnings to the Madison Surgery Center about the conscience rights of medical professionals as well as the legal concerns about public funding for abortion had thrown a monkey wrench into the plan. We continued with regular small-scale vigils in front of the building, but by the time summer rolled around, we knew it was time for another large event. Vigil for Life and Pro-Life Wisconsin decided to work together on another rally.

Initially, we planned to meet up at the Madison Surgery Center. As I talked with Matt Sande, however, I had another idea.

"Matt, we're always at the Madison Surgery Center," I said. "We will keep going there on a daily basis, but I wonder if we might have a bigger impact if we go to Meriter. Let's make them feel the pain a little bit." Just as we did with the forty-hour vigil at the university hospital, we wanted to take our opposition right to the doorstep of the Meriter decision makers.

On June 17, more than 120 prayer warriors met in front of Meriter, stretching the entire block of the hospital's main entrance. Hospital officials learned of our vigil in advance. By this time, an email from the Meriter media relations department instructing employees to "please avoid talking to protesters" had been released. Not only did Meriter have a public relations problem with the general public but also had an internal problem with its own staff. Pro-life doctors ignored the directive. Instead, they came out to the street and walked down the line of prayer volunteers, shaking hands and thanking each of them for their witness and their persistence.

The rest of the summer passed largely uneventfully. Still underemployed, I grew in my faith by taking Peter, now two years old, to daily Mass each morning. Once or twice a week, we'd follow Mass with an hour in prayer in front of the Madison Surgery Center.

I would have benefited from about two more hands. I pushed Peter in his stroller up the street with my forearms, using my left hand to hold a sign facing traffic. I used my right hand to finger my rosary beads. I continued around the corner until I reached the end of the property, turned around, and switched the rosary beads to the left hand and the sign to the right. It wasn't the most graceful sight, but it did the job.

As is the case in many college towns, the University of Wisconsin campus is, perhaps, the most liberal part of a liberal town. My presence usually drew more middle fingers than thumbs up. When the traffic light stopped the flow of

cars, it wasn't uncommon for morning commuters to sere-
nade me with a profane tirade. To verbally attack me was
one thing. To do it in front of a two-year-old seemed entirely
over the line.

Nevertheless, I had learned to exercise patience amidst
the hatred and hoped that a humble, Christlike response
would send a stronger message than any verbal response I
could muster. The more time I spent on the sidewalk, the
more I developed an awareness that the most scathing
responses were driven by the pain of having experienced
abortion. The only time I remember feeling unnerved was
when one driver rolled down his window and punctuated
his outburst by pointing to my son in the stroller and yelling,
"Nice prop!"

On a couple of occasions, our volunteers displayed
graphic images depicting the bodies of children killed by
late-term abortions. Such images are controversial even
within the pro-life community, with some pro-lifers insist-
ing upon their use and others opposing them in any situation. I tended to take a position sure to offend both parties.

We made a point not to display graphic images at
Planned Parenthood during 40 Days for Life or our other
year-round vigils. The signs were not conducive to bringing in new prayer warriors, and we wanted to keep our vigil
site family friendly. Furthermore, I was concerned that their
presence would impede the healing of post-abortive women
who came to pray with us. Lastly, we wanted to remain
approachable to members of the community and to Planned
Parenthood clients.

But the Madison Surgery Center was a different situation. Again, we kept the signs away during large gatherings,
but we felt that, on occasion, it was appropriate to remind

the ivory tower administrators what "reproductive health care" actually looks like.

On one occasion, an offended passerby called the police. An officer showed up and ordered us to put our signs away. If we refused, he would hit us with a disorderly conduct citation. Fortunately, I had Matt Bowman's phone number saved in my cell phone. I spent the next ten minutes engaging the officer in one of the more awkward conversations I've been a part of. I asked Matt what to tell the officer. He told me what to say, and I relayed the message to the police officer, who was also on the phone with his supervisor. The officer told the supervisor what I said, and the supervisor told him what to tell me.

In the end, the Madison Police Department wouldn't budge. We put our signs away rather than face a ticket. We could always sue the city for suppressing our right to free speech later. And when we warned the police department that a lawsuit was forthcoming, we received an apology and a promise that we wouldn't be harassed again. The police even pledged to make sure the rookie officer was properly trained on such a First Amendment issue. I suspect the police department forgot that the rookie officer was taking direct orders from his supervisor!

I would love to claim that my regular vigils in front of the Madison Surgery Center were driven by a heroic, saintly love for God and neighbor. In reality, I hated going out to the sidewalk. In fact, I generally celebrated rainy days because I knew it would be irresponsible to take a toddler out in inclement weather. But I had made a promise that we'd show up to pray in front of the would-be abortion center as long as it took, and I wasn't about to give up. Besides, others were making far greater sacrifices than I was. My drive into town took fifteen or twenty minutes. Some volunteers drove more than an hour when they came to pray each week. When the *Wisconsin State Journal* profiled several of the regular prayer warriors in the newspaper, those who were business owners faced blowback and risked financial retribution from a largely pro-abortion community.

SUSAN

But perhaps the most courageous gesture on the sidewalk came from a woman named Susan, who found herself on the receiving end of one abortion supporter's blistering tirade. When folks driving to work heckled us, we were assured the encounter only lasted as long as the red light. But confrontations with pedestrians were always a bit more unpredictable. And when a passerby got up in a prayer warrior's face to unleash a vicious verbal attack, actual physical violence seemed possible.

Susan stepped in between the prayer warrior and the angry passerby and asked meekly, "I had my abortion in 1972. When did you have yours?" Those words changed everything. The woman who had been berating our vigil participant stopped immediately, collapsing into Susan's arms, sobbing. From her own experience with abortion, Susan knew the pain that was driving this woman's anger. She knew it firsthand. But while both women on the sidewalk that morning had experienced the trauma of abortion, there was one key difference: instead of allowing unresolved grief to turn into anger, Susan offered her pain to the Lord, allowing Him to transform it into love. And in doing so, she diffused a volatile situation while witnessing to the love of Christ to a sister desperately in need of it.

Though we didn't spend a great deal of time together, I learned a lot from Susan. She had grown up in an abusive home and, as an adolescent, became pregnant by means of a sexual assault. Knowing that news of her pregnancy would lead to more abuse at home, she arranged a flight across the country to one of the few states where abortion was legal prior to the *Roe v. Wade* Supreme Court decision of 1973. She immediately regretted her decision. "I knew it was wrong," Susan told me. "I'm a peaceful person."

The abuse she received growing up as well as her abortion experience gave Susan a keen insight on how violence perpetuates violence. Her family history was riddled with abortion, and she desperately wanted to find a way to break the cycle.

That desire became significantly more difficult when Susan's niece learned she was pregnant and scheduled what would be her second abortion. Susan did everything she could to change the niece's mind, but to no avail. Knowing that her niece's father would be the one to bring his daughter to the abortion appointment, Susan pleaded with her brother. Though he was aware that abortion was not a positive solution to his daughter's crisis pregnancy, he was resigned to it as being the most tolerable option available. He knew abortion was wrong. He knew it would hurt his daughter. But he couldn't bring himself to believe there was enough love in the world to bring the best out of an admittedly difficult situation.

As hope grew dim, I approached Susan with one last idea. "What if Laura and I offered to adopt the baby? Do you think that might help?"

I knew that many abortion-minded women don't consider adoption because they can't stomach the thought of someone else raising their child. But I hoped that, because Susan knew us, her niece might find the idea a little more palatable. Open adoption, closed adoption, we didn't care. A child needed a home, and we would be delighted to provide that home.

Susan thought this was an excellent idea. She thought there was at least a fair chance that her niece might take us up on the offer. We didn't know what the odds were, but we couldn't help but to consider the joy we would have in our family of three becoming a family of four. As we awaited a response from Susan's niece, we quietly envisioned what the future might hold for the Karlens and a new arrival.

Ultimately, that response we were waiting for never came. Susan's niece broke off communication, and days later, she went through with the abortion. Laura and I were heartbroken. Other than Susan's optimism, there was no indication our offer would be accepted, but even from many miles away, we had begun to form a bond with this child in our hearts.

Susan, of course, was even more devastated. Her dream of breaking the cycle of abortion in her own family suffered another setback, and she knew the pain of her niece's abortion would linger for many years. Only months later, this premonition proved tragically prophetic when Susan's brother suffered a massive heart attack and passed away. "My brother died of a broken heart," she would say.

ON-THE-GROUND INTELLIGENCE

One of the big benefits of a near-daily presence in front of the Madison Surgery Center was that we were able to gather intelligence. Occasionally, a prayer volunteer had the opportunity to discuss the abortion plan with a doctor or even a high-level administrator. These conversations were always brief and rarely went into detail, but they did provide us a glimpse of what was going on behind the scenes.

While the Madison Surgery Center was publicly silent on when the plans would go into effect, we noted minor developments that we worried signaled the imminent implementation of the abortion plan. Signage appeared, warning prayer warriors and protesters about the city's trespassing ordinances. So, too, did a series of surveillance cameras across the property. I liked to joke that if the Madison Surgery Center officials wanted to use their budget to watch us pray the rosary, it was their prerogative.

It also appeared that construction was being done on the facility. Could it be related to the abortion plan? Some of our concerns were admittedly speculative, but to be as vigilant as possible, we noted every development. In late August, we confirmed that abortions were scheduled to begin in September.

In September, however, the script suddenly flipped, and reports emerged that the Madison Surgery Center was having second thoughts about opening the late-term abortion center. Rumors swirled that an overwhelming number of health-care professionals were refusing to assist in the performance of abortions. Indeed, almost all of the Madison Surgery Center's nearly one hundred staff members signed written statements refusing to participate.[1] Then, a source deep within Meriter reported that the late-term abortion plans might, themselves, be aborted. This was no slam dunk. Our source estimated it was still a 50-50 chance that the abortions would take place, but we felt more confident than we had in months.

When football season began, we handed out leaflets to folks walking across campus to the stadium. Certainly, some Badger fans got mad. It didn't bother me. Anger, I could understand. This was a contentious issue. Perhaps, the anger was rooted in the pain of a personal experience with abortion. But whatever the motivation, at least the anger demonstrated that we were engaging members of the community, forcing them to confront the reality of late-term abortion.

The more troubling response was apathy.

"Is this about abortion?"

"Yes, sir, the University of Wisconsin health system is planning to open a late-term abortion center in this building."

"Not interested. I'm here to watch football."

That kind of response made *me* angry.

You've got three and a half hours to watch guys run into each other, I thought. *Is it too much to ask to take thirty seconds to consider a matter of life and death?*

Thankfully, some fans took our presence seriously. I handed a flyer to one man who stopped and read it thoroughly. His eyes filled with anger, and I suspected he was about to let me have it. But when he responded, I realized the emotion on his face wasn't anger toward me. It was the same devastating horror I experienced when I learned of my alma mater's involvement in a late-term abortion scheme.

"Is this real?" he said.

"Yes, I'm afraid it is," I responded.

He walked away, devastated, too stunned to say more. I think I ruined his day.

A GREATER SACRIFICE

Our fall 40 Days for Life campaign was set to begin on September 23, and we had a decision to make. Would we return to Planned Parenthood, or would we hold our vigil at the Madison Surgery Center? Ultimately, to try to save as many lives as possible, we decided we needed to go to Planned Parenthood where abortions were being performed. That decision was made easier by the knowledge that Pro-Life Wisconsin's Dane County affiliate—including Jeanne who made the sign that got me kicked out of the college basketball pre-game show—would continue to maintain a regular witness near campus.

We launched our fall campaign by hosting a kickoff event a week and a half before day 1. Even though we would be praying at Planned Parenthood, the situation downtown remained on everyone's mind. I provided an update in which I told participants that the pro-life medical personnel at the Madison Surgery Center were doing their best to obstruct the abortion plan and that we needed to continue supporting them. Momentum was on our side, and we had a real chance to prevent these late-term abortions from taking place.

Those remarks were picked up by the local Catholic radio station, leading to an anonymous phone call from a man who said he was the husband of one of the pro-life doctors at the Madison Surgery Center. His voice saturated with emotion, he told me how much our support mattered and urged us to keep up our presence. "Keep going," he pleaded. "Keep it up!"

As we got deeper into September, I became increasingly convinced that we needed to do everything we could to tip the 50-50 odds in our favor. It was time to pull out all the stops. We scheduled another public rally in front of the

Madison Surgery Center for September 22—the eve of our 40 Days for Life campaign. I told volunteers this might be our last chance to prevent abortions from taking place near campus, and I believed it was true.

In some ways, our rally was a risky decision. Heading into forty straight days of around-the-clock prayer, we didn't want to start burning folks out before we even began. And we also risked poor turnout for our rally from folks saving themselves for the campaign. Nevertheless, I felt the risk was greater in not proceeding, and we forged ahead.

I hadn't looked at a weather report all week, and skies were overcast as we gathered. I grew anxious that rain might cut our event short. We had invited Fr. Rick Heilman to lead us in prayer, and, when he took the megaphone to open us in prayer, the first few drops of rain began to sprinkle.

"Oh no, Lord!" I prayed. "Don't let it rain."

A few moments later it began to rain steadily.

"Lord, this event is so important! Please stop the rain!"

The skies opened up, and a torrential downpour began.

"Please stop this rain, Lord! Otherwise all our prayer warriors are going to head for their cars as soon as Fr. Rick finishes praying."

Fr. Rick saw things differently.

"We thank You, Father, for sending us this rain because it means we have the opportunity to make a greater sacrifice for You!"

The crowd was inspired! By the time we left *hours* later, every participant was soaked from head to toe. But our presence in the middle of a monsoon sent a powerful message to the community. No longer could we be dismissed as a front group for malevolent political ideologues. Nobody would stand out in the pouring, cold September rain because he or she enjoys trampling women's rights. Only authentic love for God and neighbor could motivate the more than one hundred crazy prayer warriors to spend their entire morning getting soaked.

It seemed the tide began to turn that day. Members of the public who despised us had to respect the commitment they witnessed. Even members of the local media seemed to trust us more than they had previously. Thank God that the Lord didn't answer my prayer to stop the rain!

13

Somebody Call a Doctor

∽∽∾

The torrential rainfall at the outset of our 40 Days for Life campaign was a sign of things to come. Precipitation fell on our prayer warriors on exactly half the days of our vigil. Still, our volunteers demonstrated admirable resilience through a little bit of snow, a lot of rain, and even a hailstorm.

Near the midpoint of the campaign, I reached a disappointing milestone: the one-year anniversary of being without a full-time job. Some opportunities had arisen. I was offered a potentially lucrative sales job and turned it down. I was also a finalist for another position before I withdrew my name for consideration. But the more deeply Laura and I invested ourselves in Madison's pro-life movement, the more I believed the Lord was preparing me for full-time work. In the event that I was wrong, I kept my ear to the ground for employment opportunities, but my job search wasn't nearly as rigorous as it had been earlier in the year. Finances were tight, but with Laura working, our need wasn't imminent. We decided to stay the course and see what God had planned for us.

Fortunately, I wasn't entirely without work. Shortly after I found myself unemployed, David—the 40 Days for Life volunteer whose gloves saved me from frostbite in front of the Madison Surgery Center—approached me about a part-time job opportunity. He knew I was seeking a job and that my first position out of college involved fund-raising and donor development, so he asked whether I might be interested in doing similar work for a startup clinic that was coming to Madison.

OUR LADY OF HOPE CLINIC

A pro-life family physician named Michael Kloess had recently learned about a Catholic medical practice in Modesto, California. The providers at this clinic opt out of the traditional insurance-based practice. Instead, the clinic operates on donations. Patient-benefactors contribute the operating funds in the form of annual donations based on age and family size. In return for their support, patient-benefactors receive concierge medical care. This means around-the-clock access to a personal physician, same-day clinic visits, and thirty-minute appointments (compared with a national primary-care average of only five to seven minutes), all at no charge beyond the annual donation. These perks ensure improved health care through a truly personal relationship with one's physician.

Concierge health care had become trendy on both the East and West Coasts as well as some metropolitan areas, particularly among wealthy patients who don't want to settle for the "managed care" model their insurance programs cover. Because concierge-based medicine doesn't bill insurance—notably government insurance programs like Medicare and

Medicaid—clinics aren't bogged down by tedious federal reporting requirements. That means low overhead and lucrative margins.

In founding their practice, the doctors in Modesto weren't looking to get rich, however. They were looking to practice health care consistent with their faith. Under this innovative model, patient-benefactors comprise a little less than half of a clinic's patient base. The majority of the patient base consists of uninsured members of the community welcome to receive their care free of charge.

This model serves as a modern manifestation of a Catholic health-care tradition that goes back centuries. It isn't merely members of the upper and middle classes donating funds to provide a clinic for the poor. It is the upper, middle, and working classes helping to provide for the poor at the *same* clinics where they receive their own health care. People from all walks of life can visit the doctor in true solidarity.

Furthermore, the Modesto clinic provides 100 percent pro-life health care: no abortions or abortion referrals, no physician-assisted suicide, no contraception or sterilizations. It also provides natural family planning (NFP) services to help families space or achieve pregnancy naturally and ethically. This is authentically Catholic, authentically Christian health care.

Dr. Kloess decided he wanted to adopt this model of health care, and he moved his family across Wisconsin to give it a shot. He formed a board of directors, incorporated Our Lady of Hope Clinic, and set out to recruit patient-benefactors from around the Madison area.

In many ways, his timing couldn't have been better. While President Obama never seriously pursued the Freedom of Choice Act he championed as a candidate, he did spend the first fourteen months of his presidency pushing through sweeping health-care legislation that dramatically changed the practice of medicine in America.

Washington, D.C.'s vision for health care represented the polar opposite of Dr. Kloess's vision. Rather than promoting a stronger doctor-patient relationship, the 2,700-page law centralized the way health-care decisions are made through a long list of onerous mandates on both insurance companies and consumers. Moreover, the president's proposal ultimately subsidized health insurance plans that cover elective abortions and required insurance plans to cover contraception—even abortifacient contraception.[1]

Our Lady of Hope Clinic provided a welcome alternative. Not only was the clinic model pro-life, but Dr. Kloess was also a Creighton Model FertilityCare System NFP medical consultant, meaning that he was trained to use his NFP expertise to diagnose and treat a myriad of women's health problems morally instead of simply using birth control pills to mask symptoms.

Dr. Kloess now needed to recruit enough patient-benefactors to open the doors. That's when David from our 40 Days for Life campaign—one of the clinic's board members—offered the job to me. My mission, should I choose to accept it, would be to recruit up to six hundred patient-benefactors in order to make the clinic self-sufficient.

I wouldn't start from scratch. There were already a little more than two dozen benefactors—mostly the board of directors, their family members, and their friends. And I wouldn't need to figure out how to bring these benefactors on board. David had put together a comprehensive development plan, centered on small-group home gatherings and presentations at local churches. If all went according to plan, the temporary position would last four to six weeks before a full complement of benefactors eliminated the need for my role.

Laura and I had mixed feelings about the offer. At only fifteen hours a week for four to six weeks, it certainly was not a long-term solution for our family. Furthermore, it would mean we'd have to put Peter in daycare part time. Laura was pretty adamantly opposed to that.

But I saw things differently. My first two jobs had both ended unsuccessfully, and I felt I needed to shake things up. Maybe working for the clinic wasn't a long-term solution, but it could be a stepping-stone. God willing, I'd succeed in recruiting benefactors, building both my résumé and my skill set. I managed to persuade Laura of the job's merits and started a couple weeks later.

My first home gathering went well as I signed on my very first benefactor. But before long, I realized that David's development plan, while theoretically sound, was wildly optimistic. The idea of the clinic tested well with focus groups, but area residents—even those who believed strongly in the mission—proved extremely reluctant to make major changes to their health care. And in a local economy dominated by state and university employees, a lot of my prospects already had outstanding health benefits through their jobs. Furthermore, the fact that the clinic didn't bill insurance confused a lot of folks.

"Does this work with my Medicare?"

"Well, no sir. As I mentioned, Our Lady of Hope doesn't bill insurance. But that's ok because your annual contribution covers all your care here for free. Neither you nor your insurance provider will be charged a dollar. Does that make sense?"

"Yes, but what I want to know is will you take my Medicare?"

Another big challenge in recruiting was the fact that the clinic was still theoretical. Early on, I was trying to sell people on a clinic that hadn't actually opened—and, in fact, couldn't open until I could sell enough people on it! The most challenging part of every presentation came when I took questions at the end.

"This sounds like a great idea. Where is your clinic located?"

"We don't have a building yet, but we're looking at an office on the West Side near the mall!"

"Oh, . . . sounds interesting."

A couple weeks in, it became clear that the four-to-six-week development plan was looking more like a four-to-six-*year* development plan. Desperate for some success, I invited as many friends as possible to hear my pitch. Most of them accepted the invitation, probably out of pity. Not many demonstrated serious interest in signing up.

The board of directors could see that I was doing a thorough job and decided to retain me even after I finished my sixth week. I aggressively pursued every lead possible. In a really good month, I might sign on half a dozen benefactors. In a bad month, perhaps only one. I expanded my work by engaging in more traditional fund-raising to compensate for our lack of patient-benefactors. People who didn't want to change doctors but still supported the mission represented an untapped source of funds.

As the clinic's only employee—even Dr. Kloess was working for free—I became the jack of all trades. When the clinic opened in April of 2009, I organized and emceed the grand opening—attended by three hundred people, including our bishop, the late Robert Morlino. I wrote and designed the newsletter. I rewrote the website and marketing materials. I landed a front-page story in the *Wisconsin State Journal* for the clinic's opening and even managed to earn Dr. Kloess and myself an invitation for an in-studio interview with Sly in the Morning, the shock jock who grilled me on the Madison Surgery Center abortion plan.

But to effectively sell the clinic to prospective benefactors, I needed to familiarize myself with the nuances of health insurance as well as how federal tax law would characterize benefactor fees. I probably learned more working for Our Lady of Hope Clinic than I did in four years of college.

Helping to get the clinic up and running became easily the most challenging job I've ever had. A less-than-half-time job might not sound that demanding, but those fifteen hours often included both nights and weekends. I sometimes joked that if a prospective benefactor wanted to meet at three in the morning one hundred miles away, I'd be there.

When the benefactors rolled in slowly, the pressure ratcheted up. I desperately wanted some measure of professional success. Plus, I had primarily pitched the clinic to my friends. I faced humiliation if I talked them into generous support for a venture that couldn't stay in business a year. Most importantly, Dr. Kloess had moved his family and staked their future on the success of the clinic. If I failed, his family would pay the price.

An additional stressor to my precarious position was that Dr. Kloess and I had entirely different personalities. I'm an extrovert in every sense of the word. Dr. Kloess is the no-nonsense type, and his blunt and honest assessments of our development efforts initially struck me as critical, aloof, or even standoffish. Though we never seriously clashed, as benefactors trickled in slowly, I always suspected that my work wasn't quite up to his expectations.

Each month, I attended the clinic's board meeting. And each month, I expected I might come home without a job. Perhaps the board would go in a different direction and replace me. Maybe the clinic would shut its doors. In November of 2009, we hit what I considered rock bottom. The grand opening of the clinic seven months earlier provided a spike in support of and interest in the clinic, but we still weren't at the level we needed to keep things going. I suspected the end was imminent.

It's often said that necessity is the mother of invention, but desperation does the job too. I wasn't a natural salesman. My upbringing in a middle-class Midwestern family formed me to be rather averse to the persistent-bordering-on-annoying level of follow-up needed to ask folks for money and convert prospects into benefactors. But the only thing more terrifying than calling folks up and asking for money was the very real specter of failure. I learned to recruit aggressively in ways I never would have been comfortable doing before. I made cold calls. I continued to check in on my leads until I received a definitive "no." I made myself a staple at Madison Chamber of Commerce and Catholic Business Association meetings. I hassled my loved ones.

Slowly, but surely, it worked. As the number of benefactors increased, we were blessed with donations and grants that made the clinic viable in its first year of existence. A $1,000 gift here or a $5,000 grant there, it all added up. A good friend even pulled some strings to land a $15,000 grant, without which I'm not sure Our Lady of Hope Clinic would have survived.

In the process, I learned to appreciate Dr. Kloess as well. At one particular event we hosted, I engaged his wife, Laura, in conversation.

"I asked Michael the other day," she said. "'Do you think Steve is frustrated?' He said, 'I don't know.'" I began to realize that Dr. Kloess wasn't being standoffish with me. We both shared a passion for the clinic; his approach just put more trust in God. I was always anxious, and what I mistook in Dr. Kloess as aloofness was really an abiding confidence that, if it were God's will for the clinic to succeed, He'd find a way to keep the doors open.

AWKWARD SILENCE

In my role with Our Lady of Hope Clinic, I found myself sitting down with business owners, community leaders, and—occasionally—leaders in Madison's medical community. I often wondered whether anybody of influence would recognize me as the guy helping to lead the campaign to stop late-term abortions at the Madison Surgery Center. Fortunately, it never became an issue—though a stranger did approach me at the grocery store to say, "Just so you know, I know who you are and what you're doing!" My defensive posture relaxed when she added, "Keep up the great work!"

I also had an amusing encounter when I hosted an information table for Our Lady of Hope Clinic following Mass at an area Catholic church. One attendee stopped by the booth and said, "Now this is a much better way to be pro-life than those idiots who held that march downtown!"

"Oh, yes. Actually, I organized that event too."

Talk about an awkward silence!

Meanwhile, Laura experienced a bit of job turbulence herself. While we were grateful that she had the opportunity to work as a bilingual office assistant at a cleaning company when I found myself out of a job, she was developing ethical reservations about her position. Many of the cleaning staff and applicants were undocumented immigrants. That didn't bother her. What did bother her was being asked to sign off on official documents containing falsified Social Security numbers. She refused the assignment.

The beginning of the end came one morning when Laura called me crying. She was opening the mail and received a check from Planned Parenthood, which unbeknownst to her had recently signed a contract with her employer.

"What do I do?" Laura asked through her tears. "I can't process this check. It's blood money!"

I agreed, and Laura refused another assignment. Her supervisor didn't understand. He told her the check wasn't a big deal. She wasn't accepting the money personally. She was merely processing the check. But Laura wouldn't budge. Unlike when I sought out advice from people I knew would tell me I could help promote embryonic stem cell research, my wife stood her ground. Her supervisor relented and found another employee to handle the account. It wasn't really a big deal to her employer, but we wondered what refusing multiple assignments on ethical grounds might portend for Laura's long-term future with the company.

Fortunately, we never needed to answer that question. While having dinner with a couple we had met at 40 Days for Life, Laura mentioned her quandary. The husband encouraged Laura to apply for a position at the insurance office that he managed. Within a few weeks, Laura accepted the position to work for a man of strong faith rather than a company that serviced Planned Parenthood and falsified documents.

Slowly, we began to realize that the Lord always seemed to provide what we need when we needed it. He didn't usually provide any more than we needed—and certainly never any earlier than we needed it. But He never dropped us.

14

If the Lord Wants This Vigil to Happen . . .

~~~

Following our September rally in the rain, news from the Madison Surgery Center ground to a halt. We heard little, even in the way of rumors, about the implementation or demise of the abortion plan.

In October, Meriter CEO Jim Woodward sent an email that was later released by Meriter staff. It stated, "It is my understanding that the MSC will soon begin providing this service and there are no plans to change direction that I am aware of." But that's all we heard.

As fall gave way to winter, we recognized that we were rapidly approaching the one-year anniversary of the Madison Surgery Center board of directors' unanimous vote. By the grace of God, not a single abortion had been performed, and, in that year, as many as 130 had been prevented. This was great reason to celebrate, but our work wasn't done yet.

I decided we should host another big rally on Library Mall—a sequel to the one at which Shawn Carney and

Dr. Haywood Robinson had spoken. I arranged for Pro-Life Wisconsin, Wisconsin Right to Life, the Diocese of Madison, the Knights of Columbus, and the Wisconsin Family Council to return as co-sponsors, and we set a date of February 6, 2010—exactly a year from the Madison Surgery Center board vote. I just needed to find a speaker who could match the enthusiasm Shawn and Dr. Robinson had provided.

I turned to the advice of a priest, who had served as my spiritual director during my brief time in Chicago. He suggested his good friend, Chris Slattery, "the most pugnacious pro-lifer" he knew.

Chris had an interesting story. As a New York-based magazine advertising representative, Chris founded Expectant Mother Care Frontline Pregnancy Center to help empower abortion-vulnerable women to choose life back in the 1980s. Serving as a high-profile pro-life activist *and* as an ad sales rep put Chris in a tough spot. Before long, he invested himself in the pregnancy help center movement full time. Eventually, his operation expanded to numerous offices and mobile units across New York City, and his work has helped empower tens of thousands of women to choose life. Chris was passionate about his mission, and he brought a true New York City intensity to saving lives. To my delight, he also agreed to bring that intensity to Madison for our rally.

While planning the rally, I encountered one logistical problem after another. We almost had to cancel the event. The previous year we anticipated four hundred attendees and were surprised by the high turnout. However, for an event involving more than five hundred participants, the City of Madison required a million-dollar insurance policy.

I invested significant time contacting insurance companies to buy a one-day event policy. The representatives with whom I spoke weren't exactly eager to insure a rally dealing with a highly controversial topic for which counterprotesters were expected. The underwriters simply didn't want to take on the risk. Just as I was about to give up hope, Pro-Life Wisconsin saved the day. As an event sponsor, its liability coverage could be extended to our event.

CHRIS FARLEY WAS PRO-LIFE

My next problem arose when I learned that my permits wouldn't keep counterprotesters from infiltrating our event. The specific permits I obtained provided for sound amplification, use of city electricity, and a march through the downtown area. But our use of Library Mall was not exclusive. We got lucky in 2009 when the abortion supporters mistakenly set up shop at the Madison Surgery Center rather than at our rally. But we knew they wouldn't make that mistake twice. Given their attempt to incite physical altercations, it seemed certain that our opponents would enter our space and disrupt our rally.

Desperate to prevent a disaster, I asked our police contact for advice.

"You could try buying some caution tape and cordoning off your rally," he said. "It wouldn't be official, but the counterprotesters might not realize that."

It was worth a shot.

With a lot more time to prepare for and promote the rally, I was optimistic that we would surpass the attendance of the previous year's rally. Ultimately, I set my expectations too high. The turnout was good, but it wasn't great.

The Madison Surgery Center simply wasn't making head-lines anymore. Pro-lifers were still engaged, but the one-year anniversary didn't move folks to bring buses full of people to Madison the way the breaking news of UWHC's decision a year ago had. Nevertheless, hundreds of people march-ing through Madison a full year later did provide another impressive show of opposition to the provision of late-term abortions right next to campus.

Plus, the unofficial caution tape worked. Rather than entering our rally, the abortion supporters marched cir-cles around the cordoned-off area, carrying massive (and bizarre) puppets. We're still not sure what the puppets were supposed to signify. The counterprotesters did bring a bull-horn with the intention of shouting down our speakers. But because they didn't have a sound amplification permit, police barred them from using it, and their attempt to dis-rupt us fizzled out.

We did get one dose of excitement when a college stu-dent climbed a podium and began taking his clothes off—in homage to a 1990s *Saturday Night Live* skit where come-dian Chris Farley (a Madison native) played the role of a more-than-a-little-overweight male exotic dancer. The stu-dent was quickly arrested. As police led him away in hand-cuffs, a pro-lifer who had been a childhood friend of Chris Farley addressed the prankster: "I knew Chris Farley, and Chris Farley was pro-life!"

I, once again, opened the event.

"They thought we'd lose interest. They thought we'd forget. They thought we'd go away," I told the crowd. "My friends, have you lost interest? Have you forgotten? Do you plan on going away?"

The crowd roared, "No!" in response to each question.

I then looked to place our cause in the context of other great human rights struggles throughout history.

> Friends, the struggle for life is a struggle we will win. History is on our side. We live in a great nation, but it's a nation that is no stranger to bitterly divisive debates over who should be considered a human being . . . . Abortion is merely the latest in a long line of these controversies. But when all is said and done, never, ever has history sided with those who seek to dehumanize a particular segment of society.

When Chris Slattery took the stage, an incredible thing occurred. Chris reminded us that the abortion supporters still marching around us were not our enemies, saying, "Our goal is to convert. That is the purpose of the pro-life movement, to win over hearts and minds and souls. . . . We are on the side of the abortionists, too—we want to convert them."[1]

With a reminder that our only enemies are the powers and principalities of darkness, he exhorted us to pray for those who sought to interrupt our event. And just like that, they left to go chant their slogans in front of the Madison Surgery Center—once again ensuring that negative attention was drawn to the university on two campus-area locations simultaneously. The palpable tension we felt after being encircled by abortion supporters broke, and Chris exhorted attendees to send flowers to Madison Surgery Center executives for Valentine's Day. He even had a system whereby attendees with last names beginning with the letters A through E would send flowers to a particular executive, last names beginning with F through J to another, and so on. "They're going to be overwhelmed with flowers," he said. "This is going to touch their hearts because they're going to realize you're not their enemy. You're sending them a bouquet of love because that's what our cause and our movement is all about."[2]

Our rally, once again, made headlines in Monday's newspaper. As the coverage continued, I received a phone call from *Wisconsin State Journal* reporter Doug Erickson. Doug covered the religion beat for the paper to mixed reviews among our faith community. For years, he was a thorn in the side of Bishop Morlino, stirring up controversies where none existed.[3] However, I felt he was generally fair in his coverage of Our Lady of Hope Clinic and our ongoing battle with the Madison Surgery Center.

Doug asked me whether I knew how many people sent flowers to the administrators at the Madison Surgery Center.

"Actually, Doug, I don't know." I responded. "We encouraged folks to do this, but we didn't create any kind of tracking system."

Thinking aloud, Doug surmised that he could ask UW officials directly, before acknowledging that he probably wouldn't get an honest answer there. This was a brief, rather insignificant conversation, but one I felt pointed to a larger truth. An influential member of the mainstream media trusted me to provide an honest answer, but he knew he'd receive spin and talking points from the folks running the Madison Surgery Center. The integrity of our pro-life prayer warriors was well regarded.

A LEAP OF FAITH

Over the course of 2009, we continued to develop Vigil for Life as an organization. Initially, the infrastructure consisted of an email list and a checking account that lacked significant funds. Behind the scenes, I had worked to incorporate the organization and to build a board of directors.

Our Lady of Hope Clinic graciously provided its waiting room for our after-hours December meeting. We needed to try to figure out a way to break the stalemate with the Madison Surgery Center once and for all, and Laura had an idea.

"I think we should apply to lead the spring 40 Days for Life campaign," she said.

We had passed on the spring campaign the year before, afraid to burn out our volunteers, and I thought we should do the same in 2010. After all, the spring 40 Days for Life campaign coincides with Lent each year. Perhaps that's a spring campaign in Texas, where 40 Days for Life started, but in the upper Midwest, the first campaign of the year is most assuredly a *winter* campaign! This year's would be particularly early with Ash Wednesday on February 17.

"Laura, there's no way. It's going to be too cold. There's still no parking. Everybody is still exhausted from the fall campaign. Remember how it rained, snowed, and hailed for twenty of the forty days?"

My wife wasn't convinced, so I continued my case, telling Laura that a twenty-four-hour campaign at Planned Parenthood was one thing, but it wouldn't be safe down by campus. And without going around the clock, how would volunteers retrieve and stow their signs, the sign-in sheet, and the prayer supplies that we had always kept on site?

Laura *still* wasn't convinced. I continued to press the point, perhaps as much to justify myself as to persuade her.

"We've been running our volunteers so hard with rallies and vigils and demonstrations. Not only will we not have enough volunteers, but we'll also wear folks down so much that they won't want to come back for the annual fall campaign at Planned Parenthood!"

Laura patiently took my best shots, and then she offered one of her own. "Steve, you might be right. We might *not* get the volunteers we need. Maybe we'll do twelve days for life, run out of people, and go home," she admitted. "But if the Lord wants this vigil to happen, He's going to send us the people to make it happen. And besides, I don't think the university health system can withstand forty straight days of us praying in front of its building all day."

How could I argue with that?

I couldn't. I dropped my opposition, and our newly formed board of directors voted to apply for the spring campaign.

That's not to say I was gracious or courageous about it. I actually insisted that Laura lead the campaign rather than me because the prospect of a second forty-day vigil still overwhelmed me. I would help, of course, but I didn't feel I was up for the responsibility of being in charge of the vigil. Even though Laura was working a full-time job, she remained undaunted and faithfully spent her lunch hour every day making calls and organizing the campaign.

As we progressed toward the spring campaign, I found myself battling what I would later come to believe were spiritual attacks as a small number of supporters sharply criticized my leadership. One of our volunteer coordinators emailed me to complain about my leadership of the February rally, which he felt was too confrontational. I've never been a big fan of settling disputes over email, so I called him. He felt my opening remarks ("Have you lost interest? Have you forgotten? Do you plan on going away?") were inflammatory. When I politely disagreed, he acknowledged that perhaps a pep rally-style of event just didn't appeal to him, but the feedback was still discouraging.

I also managed to alienate some of the rally attendees when the musician who kicked off the event played exclusively Catholic music—much to the chagrin of the heavily Protestant membership of one of the event co-sponsors.

The most stinging rebuke came from one of our most dedicated leaders—a man who had made heroic sacrifices in defense of life as well as in solidarity with the poor. He had asked me for help on a specific pro-life project he was working on. I said yes out of vanity. I didn't want to disappoint anybody by saying no. Ultimately, I realized I might not be able to make good on my promise, and my failure to come through for my friend upset him much more than had I simply said no from the start. "I'm not mad," he said, "but you lack integrity as a leader because you don't keep your promises, and I'm not going to work with you anymore."

I fumed. The attacks from the abortion industry didn't bother me. That's what we had signed up for. But when I felt I was being attacked by my own side, I became livid. As a pro-life acquaintance once said, "The arrows in the back hurt worse than the arrows in the front."

"Can't these people see how hard I'm working—all as a volunteer?" I asked Laura. "I'm doing the best that I can!" I even entertained quitting. "If this isn't good enough, then maybe I should just spend my time doing something else!"

In hindsight, it's easy to see that our fallen nature allowed insignificant disagreements to fester. The criticism I received wasn't always wrong. After all, I had not even been in the pro-life movement for two years. And once I got involved, I took on a leadership role almost immediately. I was young and inexperienced. Sometimes, it showed. That's not to say my critics always reacted fairly, but they, too, were only human.

It's this realization that led me to quit feeling sorry for myself and to get back to work. All of our volunteers were sinners. All of us had flaws. If I wanted folks to be patient with me, I needed to be patient with them. Recognizing that the number of volunteers with whom I butted heads was small and that all of them were good people, I came to suspect that the devil was trying to derail us. I posted on my Facebook page, "The amount of spiritual warfare going on around here leads me to believe we're on to something."

Indeed, we were. As we drew near to kicking off the campaign, the rumor mill started to churn once again. We received a report from a medical specialist that the Madison Surgery Center decided not to pursue its abortion plan. Could this report be true? After more than a year of delays, we were *cautiously* optimistic. Then, we received a second report when a doctor who attended church with one of our vigil participants provided us with an update: "UW Health isn't going ahead with the abortions," he told Laura, "but they're not going to admit it publicly."

It was up to us to find a way to force UWHC into an admission. I was quite uncomfortable with the idea of declaring victory—even quietly—until we had such an admission. If we packed up and went home or packed up and moved our regular vigils to Planned Parenthood, it would give UWHC officials exactly what they wanted. Under the cover of our absence, they'd be able to swoop in and begin performing late-term abortions without public opposition. Wanting to make sure we didn't crush our volunteers' motivation to join our upcoming 40 Days for Life campaign at the Madison Surgery Center, we decided not to share the apparent abandonment of the late-term abortion plan. Perhaps, the upcoming campaign would help finish the plan off once and for all.

We decided to run our campaign from 6:00 a.m. to 6:00 p.m. every day, and our first task was to figure out where to store our supplies. Fortunately, a Catholic church only a few blocks away provided us with access to a storage bin on the property. Every weekday, Ron Faust, a state-level leader for the Knights of Columbus and one of the men whose tremendous commitment to 40 Days for Life led me to join the Knights, and my old friend Adam Morse took the first hour of the day, ensuring that the supplies made it to the vigil without confusion. Their sacrifice was one of the major, but unsung, contributions that made our campaign possible. We were also blessed with a pool of volunteers who helped us store and retrieve supplies by regularly covering the last hour of each day as well as the first hours every Saturday and Sunday.

Anyone who's ever led a 40 Days for Life campaign will tell you the most stressful part of the campaign cycle takes place well before day 1. Volunteers have a tendency to wait until the last minute to commit to signing up for hours. Our campaign at the Madison Surgery Center was no different. Two weeks prior to the campaign, a nearly empty vigil schedule needing nearly one thousand hour-long prayer commitments was a terrifying sight.

Laura and I resorted to the desperation tactic we had perfected when we led the previous campaign. We called it the "Damsel-in-Distress Method." I'd review the schedule, the hours we needed, and volunteers who were typically available for those hours. And then I'd feed names and phone numbers to Laura so she could make the calls. We found this approach to be efficient. But more so, we found that, as a woman, Laura's pleas for help were more successful than mine. It turns out that our male volunteers stepped up to the plate not only to protect children in danger and abortion-minded women but also to come to the rescue for the working mom who needed to fill her vigil calendar.

Even so, we made it a few days into the vigil, and things were not looking good. Our schedule was a disaster, and it looked like Laura's quip about completing 12 Days for Life might have even been on the optimistic side. In what was becoming an annual event, Laura tearfully called Fr. Heilman and begged his help mobilizing the Knights of Divine Mercy. Fr. Rick and his men came through once again, and the vigil coverage improved quickly.

Another key to our vigil was Jeanne, who—with her wagon full of signs in tow—officially signed up for sixty hours during the forty days. This was a record for the Madison campaign. Unofficially, Jeanne spent many more hours at the vigil than she took credit for.

We closed our 40 Days for Life campaign on Palm Sunday. In spite of my certainty that we would never have enough volunteers and the rough start, we ultimately filled the schedule more easily than we ever had before. Our closing vigil in front of the would-be abortion center saw hundreds of pro-lifers come out to pray as Fr. Heilman led us in the Stations of the Cross.

The Lord answered this same prayer to put the strip club across the street from Fr. Heilman's church out of business. Maybe He'd bless us by ending the Madison Surgery Center's late-term abortion scheme.

15

No More Sunsets

~~~

As soon as I heard Laura burst through the bathroom door that sunny April morning, I knew she was pregnant. I hadn't yet opened my eyes, but I didn't need to. Her footsteps told me everything.

My wife didn't have any particular reason to believe she might be pregnant, but after years of praying for a second child, I'd grown accustomed to Laura taking random pregnancy tests—hoping against hope that somehow that second pink line would appear.

This time it did.

Throughout our engagement, I had grappled with the question of contraception. Like many young Catholics, I had grown up with a vague awareness that my faith frowned upon contraception, but I didn't understand why. I didn't care to either. It was simply much easier to parrot mindless talking points about "celibate, old men" having no right to discuss marital intimacy than to inquire why the Church taught what it taught.

I got my first dose of truth while at college. Dr. Janet Smith was a guest speaker at the Catholic center on campus, and she gave a brilliant talk about the dangers of birth control. I left thoroughly convinced—for a while, at least. But it didn't take long for the cares of the world to lead me astray again. Before long, I began repeating the same tired platitudes about God not expecting every family to have fifteen children. Plus, everybody used contraception. What would families do without it?

THE AUTHENTICITY OF OBEDIENCE

Toward the end of the summer of 2004, I was at home when the bishop removed our parish priest from ministry as a pastor. That priest also was a close personal friend who officiated at our wedding two years later. My friend did not respond to his removal gracefully. He refused his new assignment, found work outside the Church,[1] and sued the diocese, his religious order, and others.[2] Though I remained close to him until his death several years later, his insubordination to the bishop and his order superiors tore apart our parish community. Angry meetings were hosted at the church with riled-up parishioners threatening to "name names" of the fellow pewsitters they believed responsible for the priest's ouster. By the time the smoke cleared, many members of our Catholic community—including numerous trustees and parish council members—had left the parish.[3] Dozens of students left the parish school.[4] Some publicly discussed leaving the Catholic Church entirely.[5] Some of those who left went on to form a splinter group centered on promoting their vision of a more "progressive" Catholicism.[6]

Because of our relationship with our pastor, my family considered leaving too. But, ultimately, we recognized that our faith went beyond one personality and we stayed. Slowly, the church grew back, even if the folks who left angrily never returned. Months later, a deacon who remained preached the homily for the Sunday Mass. After acknowledging that recent events had made for a trying and painful time in the parish, he spoke of his reason for silently enduring the difficult ordeal without going on the offensive as so many others had. "When I was ordained, I took a vow of obedience to the bishop," he simply said, adding that it was a vow he intended to keep.

His message was simple, and more than a decade and a half later, I might be the only person who remembers it. But it resonated with me. We live in a world where self-assertion is the norm. Dissent and protest are a part of everyday life. Authority is viewed with scorn. Deacon Dave's pledge to remain obedient wasn't a sign of weakness. I saw it as a sign of courage and of authenticity.

This simple act of obedience stayed with me through my engagement, and I began to waver in my intent to involve contraception in our marriage. I still wasn't sure that contraception was wrong, but the prospect of risking both my soul and the soul of my beloved left me increasingly ill-at-ease.

Laura had talked of waiting at least a few years before we had children, so it took me a little time to work up the nerve to initiate the conversation. For some reason, I decided the grocery store parking lot was the right place.

"Laura, I've got some moral concerns about birth control," I said sheepishly. "I'm not sure we should use it."

"That's fine," she replied.

"Really? You're not upset? You don't think I'm crazy?"

"No, I don't."

And that was that.

We got married in late June 2006. Two weeks earlier, doctors told Laura she wouldn't be able to have babies. One month into marriage, Laura was pregnant with Peter. To this day, I believe that God blessed us with Peter the first year of our marriage in response to our fidelity regarding the Church's teachings on contraception. Of course, Laura immediately fell in love with Peter and questioned why she had ever considered waiting years to have children. We anticipated having a huge Catholic family, not because there were no moral ways to space children but because of the desire to have even more little human beings to love.

This grandiose vision wasn't to be. Each month was met with disappointment, and Dr. Kloess at Our Lady of Hope Clinic soon confirmed a diagnosis of polycystic ovarian syndrome, which we long suspected Laura had. Her previous doctors failed to address her condition at its root. Instead, they were content to mask symptoms by prescribing the birth control pill. The opportunity to work with Dr. Kloess brought us hope that we might eventually be blessed with more children. But, before he even had the chance to help, the surprise pregnancy test brought us good news.

The days ahead were as joyful as any we had experienced in our life together. We beamed when friends who knew of our struggle with secondary infertility congratulated us, and we devoured all the fetal development materials we could find, eager to mark every milestone in our baby's nascent life. We even sent a message to the entire Vigil for Life email list because so many of our prayer warriors had kept our desire for a baby in prayer.

GIANNA

Whenever Laura starts a conversation with the words, "I hope you don't mind," I know something interesting is sure to follow. Laura finished her mysterious introduction: "but I promised the Lord that if He blessed us with a child, we'd name the baby John Paul or Gianna."

I had no complaints. John Paul would honor the man who, until his death only five years earlier, had served as pope for our entire lives. A pro-life hero who stood up to both the Nazi occupation and the Soviet regime, "JP2" was one of the greatest saints of the past millennium.

The name Gianna would honor St. Gianna Beretta Molla, who heroically refused cancer treatment while pregnant with her fourth child. In doing so, she sacrificed her life so that her pre-born daughter might live. St. Gianna's popularity was growing in the pro-life movement, and we had the opportunity to meet her son at a conference the previous summer. Laura and I decided we'd pray a novena asking for St. Gianna's intercession for our pregnancy—nine days of prayer that concluded on her feast day, April 28.

Celebrating Peter's third birthday at Chuck E. Cheese a few days after the positive pregnancy test, we couldn't have been happier. Among the presents he opened was the Dr. Seuss movie *Horton Hears a Who*. Reflecting on the film's signature quote, "A person's a person no matter how small," it was clear that evening our family of three had *finally* become a family of four.

A week later I remember foolishly telling Laura, "I'm sure we'll be sad again someday, but right now I just can't see how!"

It didn't take long for that statement to be fulfilled. It was another sunny spring morning —only sixteen days after the positive pregnancy test and the day after St. Gianna's feast day—when Laura realized something was wrong. Our doctor sent us to the hospital for an ultrasound to figure out what was going on. The drive was long, partly because of anxiety, partly because our boycott of Meriter Hospital meant we needed to drive to another town to find a hospital our insurance plan covered.

The ultrasound technician looked around for a few moments before declaring, "There is no baby." Our fears were confirmed. Laura was miscarrying.

"There's no baby?" she cried out before the tears began to fall. As Laura sobbed the bitter tears that only a mother who has lost a child can fully understand, the ultrasound technician asked if she wanted to talk with a counselor before we left.

"No," Laura said. "I want to talk to Fr. Rick."

In disbelief, we left the hospital to pick up Peter, stopping along the way to pray at church only to find the doors were locked. It shouldn't have come as a major surprise. Our parish wasn't far from one of the more crime-ridden parts of town. But with our dreams of welcoming a child into the world dashed, that locked door seemed to represent our hopes of raising more children.

We called Fr. Heilman, whose church was about fifteen minutes away. Without any notice, he welcomed us to his home, heard our confessions, and spoke with us at length about our sorrow.

Though it was too early to tell, Laura felt the baby was a girl, and we named her Gianna. Before bed that night, we recovered the tiny body of our baby. Suddenly, I was at the foot of the cross, helplessly consoling a sobbing mother clutching the lifeless body of her beloved child.

The script had flipped. We knew we'd be happy again someday; we just couldn't see how.

DIGGING IN DRESS SHOES

In my household, we'll forever remember April 29 as the anniversary of our miscarriage. But it's a day that also holds significance on the Catholic Church calendar as the feast of Catherine of Siena, the patron saint of miscarriage. We came to believe this feast day presents a great opportunity to rethink the way we approach miscarriages. In America, few miscarried babies are treated with the dignity that their short lives deserve. Most are thrown out with medical waste, unnamed and unacknowledged.

Even the Church today finds itself woefully unprepared to minister to couples grieving this loss. When Laura and I miscarried, we weren't quite sure what to do. Our faith taught us that our child—our Gianna—had the same dignity as any other human being. But the lack of an ecclesiastical protocol for handling a miscarriage indicated otherwise.

Fr. Mark Vander Steeg, a good friend from my home diocese, understood this well. He drove two hours to our apartment to spend a day with us. Together, he and Fr. Heilman decided to preside at a funeral Mass and Christian burial for Gianna. Fr. Heilman even provided a free burial plot on the edge of his cemetery that we could use. Still, there was a slight hiccup in the plan. This burial hadn't followed any of the typical funeral protocols, so nobody had dug the grave. It was up to me. I actually cherished the opportunity.

We weren't burying only a child; we were also burying our dreams. We would never hold this baby. Never play with her. We wouldn't get to watch her grow up and become a woman and do all the things parents dream of their children doing. In a matter of hours, all those dreams had washed away.

I wouldn't get to make sacrifices for my daughter. There would be no sleepless nights, no staying up late with a sick child, no tea parties in the dining room. I would never walk her down the aisle on her wedding day. There was only one thing I could do for Gianna and that was to dig her grave. Searching for a way to honor my daughter, I resolved to dig the best darn hole that had ever been dug.

Fr. Mark and I arrived at the church early, hung up my suit, and walked up to the cemetery. It didn't take long to find that digging the hole was not going to be easy. The ground was hard and rocky and gnarled with roots. I did my best, but I wasn't making enough progress. Fr. Mark saw me struggling and took the shovel. I was still in shorts, but I'll never forget the sight of him in his black clerical garb and polished shoes digging a grave with me in the warm May sun.

In the Catholic tradition, burying the dead is one of the seven corporal works of mercy—and perhaps the one that is the most difficult to apply in the modern world. Fr. Mark's help digging was a tremendous act of friendship. The two of us took turns with the shovel and, ultimately, came up with a suitable hole. Then we went into the church so I could get dressed and Fr. Mark could prepare for Mass.

Laura and I had gone out on a limb, inviting the entire pro-life community to the funeral. We wanted to lean on our friends during a difficult time, but we also wanted to send a message: building a true culture of life requires a greater respect for the lives of miscarried babies. Certainly, loss of a miscarried baby is a very personal experience, and not everybody goes through it the same way. But the tears and the hugs shared that evening confirmed my suspicions that parents of miscarried babies everywhere are starving for their grief to be legitimized.

This became painfully clear to me when I invited my parents to come down for the funeral. They told me they were busy that night, but I didn't feel that was an acceptable answer. They were pro-life enough to know that this tiny body was nothing less than their grandchild. Why wouldn't they come?

I was a little bit embarrassed, wondering whether I was being too dramatic in hosting the funeral and expecting family members to come. My convictions about the dignity of human life led me to ask my family to treat this child with the same love, patience, and compassion they would have if we had lost a born child. Was that asking too much? I didn't think so. After all, a person's a person no matter how small.

Unfortunately, my emotional state led to a less-than-charitable reaction in which I lashed out at my parents. It wasn't a pleasant conversation, but ultimately, they made arrangements to join us for the funeral. Later on, my mom admitted that unresolved grief from a miscarriage she suffered prior to my birth played a role in her reluctance to come. My dad simply said, "I didn't understand. But now I understand."

More than one hundred family members and friends joined us—some traveling hours to do so—to grieve Gianna that beautiful Monday evening. A few who had never even met us were moved by our story and drove a distance to share their condolences.

Fr. Heilman and Fr. Mark celebrated a beautiful liturgy, which concluded with a surprising announcement from Fr. Heilman. "It's my pleasure to announce that this summer we'll begin construction on a rosary garden where miscarried and stillborn children will be recognized and buried."

The idea had come together quickly. While preparing for Mass that evening, Fr. Mark told Fr. Heilman that he was in the process of establishing a miscarriage memorial and burial site at the church where I grew up. Such memorials were not and still are not regular fixtures in American churches, but Fr. Mark recognized the need. "It's part of the New Evangelization," he'd later say.

After Mass, we buried Gianna near the future site of the rosary garden. As we processed back toward the church, I looked back toward the cemetery, struck by the beauty of the sun setting over a nearby cornfield. Fr. Mark noticed my gaze. "One day there will be no more sunsets," he said. "Only eternal light."

We had planned to invite guests to join us at a local restaurant after the burial, but our friends planned something better yet. Jeanne and another man my wife and I knew simply from attending daily Mass provided a meal at the parish hall. They generously provided hot food for all those who came from far and wide to mourn with us. They even brought a cake, frosted with the words, "We love you, Gianna Maria Karlen."

The love of our friends and family members buoyed our spirits. The pain was still there, but, for one evening our loved ones, young and old, brought us joy. Not only was the meal impressive, but our friends took care of all the setup and the entire cleanup process. These people were truly living out our Lord's command: "Love one another."

16

Victory

~~~

On Tuesday morning, it was back to reality. Laura went back to work. I got busy trying to build the benefactor base for Our Lady of Hope Clinic and combatting the Madison Surgery Center's late-term abortion plan. It was difficult to get back in the saddle after Laura's pregnancy brought so much hope. Not only had we been expecting a baby, but the growth of our family would have meant I'd need to find full-time employment. It had seemed like we might get to have a more traditional family life and work schedule. All those hopes were only a wisp of smoke now.

I was about to start working on benefactor recruitment for the clinic when my phone rang. It was Chris Slattery. "Hey Steve, this is Chris." He continued in his thick New York accent. "I'm gonna offah you a job. You gonna come to New Yawk, be a New Yawkah."

Perhaps, Tuesday morning didn't mean business as usual after all!

After a quarter century of saving babies, Chris had decided to hire a fund-raising and development director to further expand his network of pregnancy centers. He was impressed with the work we had done fighting the late-term abortion plan in Madison, and he knew Laura and I had just lost the baby. Maybe, he said, this would be a perfect opportunity for him to grow his work *and* for Laura and me to get a fresh start. We discussed the opportunity, and I agreed to fly to Florida to meet him at the national conference for Heartbeat International—a network of affiliated pregnancy centers. This was big news for me, but it wasn't the day's biggest news.

After calling Laura and other family members, I spent a couple hours working and picked Peter up from the baby-sitter. Walking in the door to our apartment shortly before lunchtime, I noticed I had a voice mail from Matt Sande. "Hey Steve, it's Matt Sande. Call me back as soon as you get this."

Sounds urgent, I thought. *I wonder what's up.*

While I dialed Matt up, I sneaked a peak at my email and found the answer. There, at the top of my inbox, was a note from Matt Bowman: the plan to perform late-term abortions at the Madison Surgery Center had been scrapped!

"It is my understanding based on recent information from the UW that they have now abandoned plans to provide late-term abortion services at the MSC," wrote Assistant Attorney General Kevin Potter in response to a letter asking Attorney General J. B. Van Hollen to investigate the legality of the Madison Surgery Center abortion plan.[1]

For the second time that day, I got to call Laura and other family members with exciting news—and quite possibly the most gratifying news of my life. My relationship with my alma mater was damaged beyond repair; barring dramatic institutional reform, there was simply no going back. But our ragtag band of unknown, underfunded pro-life prayer warriors had won. Against all odds, the coalition of homeschooling moms, working dads, students, and senior citizens triumphed over the hospital affiliated with the University of Wisconsin, quite possibly the most powerful institution in the state.

My next order of business was to write a letter proclaiming the victory to our Vigil for Life crew—a list that now topped one thousand people. I felt it was important for them to learn the news from me before it hit the newspapers. It's not that I wanted to take credit, but after all we had been through over the previous year and a half, I wanted to celebrate the victory *together*.

And, of course, I needed to call Shawn Carney. He was delighted by the news, though I didn't get the sense he was as stunned as I was. Shawn put a great deal of faith in the power of prayer. In his eyes, the Lord's generous response to the sacrifices of His people in Madison shouldn't be shocking if we believe what we claim to believe.

Later that afternoon my phone rang, displaying an unfamiliar number from Texas. "Hey, man!" It was Dr. Haywood Robinson. "Shawn told me the good news. Congratulations!"

THE EMPIRE STRIKES BACK

Soon the entire pro-life world was celebrating the victory in Madison. But it wasn't long before UW Health attempted to spoil our fun, announcing:

> UW Health remains strongly committed to a
> comprehensive women's reproductive health service
> that includes this important procedure. . . . Because

of the sensitive nature of this clinical program, we do
not consider it in the best interests of our patients to
discuss the timing or location of these services.[2]

My ecstasy turned to dread, and I called Matt Sande.
The denial was a bluff, Matt said. The report from the attorney general's office was too clear. UW Health's announcement was merely an attempt to save face.

Matt Bowman concurred with Matt Sande's assessment,
writing:

> Some media are reporting that this statement
> DENIES that the UW is pulling the abortions out
> of [the] Madison Surgery Center. But this statement in no way denies that the UW has abandoned
> plans to do the abortions at the MSC. It just says
> UW wants to do them, generally. . . .
>
> And notice that they explicitly refuse to discuss
> the timing "or location." . . . The UW now admits
> that they are planning these abortions secretly. . . .
>
> Therefore, the UW Hospital's statement says
> that it is now officially engaged in an abortion
> cover-up. The UWHCA board is appointed by the
> legislature, they had a public hearing about this
> plan, and in 2009 they denied they had concocted
> the plan in secret.
>
> But now the UW Hospital claims it can
> withhold information from the public about doing
> late-term abortions, and avoid public scrutiny
> about whether they will comply with a multitude of
> federal and state laws. The people of [Wisconsin]
> will not allow the UW Hospital to adopt an official

policy of covering up abortion schemes that were discussed in a public meeting by a state agency.[3]

Open-records requests later showed that UWHC administrators were divided on whether to even send the statement claiming the abortion plan was still in the works. Senior Vice President for Medical Affairs Carl Getto wrote in an email, "This raises a host of questions that will need to be answered and continues to put UW in the center of the pro-life debate. . . . Why are we saying this?"[4]

My fears were further eased when Special Assistant Attorney General Kevin St. John reaffirmed the letter stating that the late-term abortion plan had been canceled. "Based on the information that the Department of Justice received from UW prior to writing this letter and information that has been confirmed subsequently, the letter is accurate."[5] St. John also added that the attorney general's office based its conclusion on a UWHC admission that it neither had nor was seeking a means for paying UW staff members to perform abortions.[6]

The evidence satisfied me, but some of our volunteers just couldn't bring themselves to believe we had won. For some time, I continued to receive messages from our prayer warriors, warning me, "not so fast." Pro-lifers scrutinized the communications from the attorney general's office and UWHC, looking for the loophole that would prove a crushing letdown was coming. The doubts held by a minority of our volunteers irked me, but we declared victory anyway and ceased holding vigils at the site. On May 7, Vigil for Life and Pro-Life Wisconsin held a joint vigil of thanksgiving. It would be the last time we prayed in front of the Madison Surgery Center.

I was overwhelmed with joy. When it came time to address the crowd, I kept my message short—and rooted in Scripture: "The Lord has done great things for us, and holy is His Name!"[7] With the formalities out of the way, it was time to celebrate our victory privately by going out to dinner with friends.

Our meal together was really one of my first opportunities to reflect on what we had been through. For sixteen months, the Lord used me—a down-and-out, underemployed father struggling to make ends meet for his young family—to help lead the battle against the Madison Surgery Center. Though I knew I needed a full-time job, I quit looking, believing the Lord might eventually place me in the pro-life movement full time. Laura believed the same and made a tremendous sacrifice by going back to work full time for more than a year and a half. All the while we pursued the mission the Lord had given us: stopping late-term abortions at the Madison Surgery Center. And the very day that mission came to its conclusion, the Lord began calling me to my next task by providing a job offer. And not only one job offer. When I told friends about the opportunity I had in New York, I received several more job offers. Ultimately, I knew the Lord had me right where He wanted me, but I couldn't help wondering, *Where were all these job offers a year ago when I needed work?*

The thought of relocating to the Bronx was exciting. It was also terrifying. I wanted to make the right decision and started asking the advice of my more experienced friends— including my friends at Pro-Life Wisconsin. Matt Sande said he had heard nothing but good things about Chris and his operation, but, first, he had a proposal for me.

"Before you go to New York, Steve, if we had a position for you here at Pro-Life Wisconsin, would you be interested?"

Having incorporated Vigil for Life, I also seriously considered an attempt at fund-raising so that we could take our local efforts full time. The thought of running an organization and working as a pro-life missionary appealed to me.

I was humbled and excited about the opportunity to go to New York, but when Laura and I learned that the cost of living meant she'd never be able to be the stay-at-home mom she desired to be, we ruled it out. I probably left Chris hanging longer than I ought to have, but it was a hard opportunity to decline. I respect him a lot, and it was difficult turning him down.

Meanwhile, I was leaning toward trying to work for Vigil for Life full time. Laura thought I belonged at Pro-Life Wisconsin. We actually spent the majority of our fourth wedding anniversary arguing about it before Laura put the decision in my hands and pledged to support me in whatever I chose. We took the matter to prayer, and as is usually the case when we disagree, God voted with Laura.

No Exceptions

Ultimately, the tide turned when I spent an afternoon helping Matt Sande move furniture. He told me about the importance of Pro-Life Wisconsin serving as the only "total protection" pro-life organization in the state. That meant that Pro-Life Wisconsin wouldn't compromise the lives of politically inconvenient children—those conceived in rape or incest or those where pregnancy endangers the life of the mother. Pro-Life Wisconsin, I came to understand, might not always be the most powerful of organizations, but it was unquestionably sincere and principled.

I thought back to our fight with the Madison Surgery Center. As state legislators considered a bill that would ban the university health system from participating in late-term abortions, some of the pro-lifers with whom we had been working argued that the legislation might stand a better chance of passing if it included an exception allowing for abortion in cases where it was necessary to save the life of the mother. They even lobbied lawmakers to include such an exception in the bill, a development that deeply troubled me.

The abortion advocates we encountered at both of our big rallies displayed a number of bizarre signs. But perhaps the most bizarre read, "Abortion bans kill women." These signs were often accompanied by the chant "Pro-life is a lie; you don't care if women die."

The pro-life coalition had done an excellent job exposing the need for a life-of-the-mother exception as a myth. We educated the public on the nuances of ethical decision making when life-threatening health conditions arose during a pregnancy.

Our position was bolstered by a quote from former U.S. Surgeon General C. Everett Koop who once stated, "Protection of the life of the mother as an excuse for an abortion is a smoke screen. In my thirty-six years in pediatric surgery, I have never known of one instance where the child had to be aborted to save the mother's life. . . ."[8] Koop's assessment wasn't only a pro-life opinion either. Back in 1967, long-time abortion advocate Alan Guttmacher wrote, "Today it is possible for almost any patient to be brought through pregnancy alive, unless she suffers from a fatal illness such as cancer or leukemia, and, if so, abortion would be unlikely to prolong, much less save, life."[9] Furthermore, resorting to abortion in the midst of a complicated pregnancy would stunt the research and development of new techniques for saving the lives of both the mother and her baby.

We weren't naïve. We recognized that sometimes treating a mother's health emergency might carry the side effect of inadvertently harming her baby. For instance, an expectant mother who undergoes chemotherapy might lose her child as an unintended side effect of her treatment. That tragic situation, however, is entirely different from directly and intentionally killing the child, which would do nothing to remedy the cancer.

We had done so much to reinforce the reality that late-term abortion is an unnecessary, brutal, and elective procedure. But now, some of the people in our coalition—people who had stood and prayed and marched with us—were essentially willing to deliver a key messaging victory to the radical pro-abortion activists by suggesting that, in medical emergencies, abortion could be a necessary act of compassion! It was a strategy I felt was shortsighted, cynical, and—above all—dangerous. And it was the perfect illustration of why our state needed an organization like Pro-Life Wisconsin.

Going full time with Vigil for Life was tempting, and going to New York was enticing. But my afternoon moving furniture with Matt reminded me that our work in Wisconsin was not done. I accepted the job offer from Pro-Life Wisconsin and started my position as director of development on July 19, 2010. In this role, I was responsible for developing the organization—both through fund-raising and by building up its county-level affiliate organizations throughout the state. Having raised money for Our Lady of

Hope Clinic and organized volunteers with Vigil for Life in Madison, the position was a perfect fit.

I couldn't wait to start, but one more hurdle remained. Pro-Life Wisconsin wasn't a large enough organization to offer an employee health benefit. *No problem*, I thought. *We'll go to Our Lady of Hope Clinic for the basics and maintain an inexpensive major medical policy to cover us should disaster strike.* It turns out it wasn't that easy. Some women with polycystic ovarian syndrome become obese and are at a significantly heightened risk of developing diabetes. Laura, in tip-top shape, was not among those women. Nevertheless, this pre-existing condition was a huge red flag to every insurance company's underwriters. We received a rejection letter informing us that she was uninsurable. We were devastated.

Our only recourse was to enroll her in the state's high-risk health insurance pool, but the cost of that was astronomically high. Freshly hired, I was going to need to find a new job—one that was full time with benefits. I had gotten so close to fulfilling the call I discerned to serve full time in the pro-life movement, and with a single letter from the insurance company, it was slipping through my hands.

As we scrambled for answers, the intercom in our apartment buzzed, indicating we had a visitor. I wasn't home, but Laura welcomed in a friend we weren't expecting to see. "One of your friends found out you were in a bit of a bind," she said. Handing Laura an envelope, she continued, "So I was asked to deliver this to you."

Laura called me in tears, recounting the unexpected visitor. The envelope contained $4,000 in cash to cover Laura's enrollment in the high-risk medical pool. I'd be able to work with Pro-Life Wisconsin after all.

Even before I started work, we received more good news. In mid-June, it was revealed that UW abortion provider Caryn Dutton, architect of the late-term abortion plan, was leaving the university, having accepted a position at Harvard.[10] It was getting more and more difficult for UW Health to claim that its late-term abortion plan was still in the works, but UW Health still wouldn't concede publicly. UWHC spokesperson Lisa Brunette said that Dutton leaving would mean "a change in who provides the service, but otherwise there is no change in our plans."[11] Internal communications at UW were more calculated. A May 20 email exchange reveals a desire to downplay Dutton's departure. "I'd make [the public statement] minimalistic," UW Medical Foundation President and CEO Jeffrey Grossman wrote. UW Medical School Dean Robert Golden concurred, "I agree with Jeff . . . 'less is more.'"[12]

It's Official

The pro-life landscape in Wisconsin changed dramatically the first week of November when Milwaukee County Executive Scott Walker and pro-life majorities in both houses of the state legislature swept into office. The new governor, lieutenant governor, senate majority leader, assembly speaker, and assembly majority leader were all endorsed by Pro-Life Wisconsin's political action committee.

On December 13—perhaps looking to ensure a good relationship with the new state government—UW Health publicly announced what we learned back in May: the late-term abortion scheme was dead.[13] The Catholics in our coalition of pro-life prayer warriors found even more meaning in the timing of the announcement. In 2010, December 13 was the transferred feast day of Our Lady of Guadalupe, the patron saint for unborn children.

In announcing the cancellation, UWHC spokeswoman Lisa Brunette couldn't resist trying to paint the faithful prayer volunteers as extremists: "We have concluded that [the Madison Surgery Center] cannot be secured to the extent necessary for patient safety and privacy."[14]

The statement was, of course, patently absurd. Thousands of pro-lifers had spent time witnessing to the sanctity of life in front of the Madison Surgery Center over the previous two years. For a year and a half, our presence on the sidewalk had been a near-daily occurrence. Not a single arrest or safety incident ever occurred. The members of the community had seen our presence again and again, in cold weather or hot, in rain, snow, sleet, or hail, over and over and over again. And even if the majority of citizens in a liberal city like Madison disagreed with us, they knew we were always on our best behavior. Nevertheless, we were gratified to see Brunette credit us for the decision to drop the abortion plan, even if she had done so dishonestly.

Shortly after the UW Health announcement, WKOW, Madison's ABC affiliate, asked to interview me about the victory, but I was meeting with Pro-Life Wisconsin supporters several hours away, and the television station wanted a live interview that day. That simply wasn't possible, so I put the reporter in touch with Laura. My wife wasn't exactly thrilled by the prospect of going on television. Laura preferred to labor behind the scenes, but, without another alternative, she agreed—as long as I would help her prepare.

The news segment couldn't have gone better. The juxtaposition between Laura and a Planned Parenthood executive representing the other side was stark. That executive awkwardly attempted to justify late-term abortion, saying, "The reason for second-trimester abortions can be really complicated. . . ."[15] Laura followed by explaining that abortion isn't some theoretical abstraction; it's violence. "It's extremely gruesome," she said. "There's no other way to put it. It's dismemberment of a baby that a few weeks later could be born out of the womb and survive."[16]

The contrast between the two was devastating for Planned Parenthood. While the Planned Parenthood official struggled to defend the indefensible, Laura ran up the score. And she was the perfect person to do it. As an attractive, articulate, and young pro-life woman, Laura was Planned Parenthood's worst nightmare. Initially, we thought the segment was aired only locally. It wasn't until a Christmas visit to out-of-town family members—who welcomed us by opening the door and shouting Laura's line, "It's gruesome! It's dismemberment!"—that we learned the broadcast must have reached a much larger audience across the state.

The following summer, we got to encounter that same Planned Parenthood executive one more time. She and Matt Sande were invited to a point–counterpoint discussion on abortion. However, Matt came down with an illness, and I was asked to step in. I was nervous to say the least. Outside of media interviews, I didn't have any experience speaking to folks on the other side of the issue. Now, I'd be facing off against an abortion industry executive.

As nervous as I was, apparently the Planned Parenthood official was more nervous. About five minutes before the event was scheduled to begin, she remarked that she wasn't going to go head-to-head with me and left. Even the abortion supporters in the room were disgusted by her decision to bail at the very last minute.

17

Life, Death, and Baseball

～～～

G od toppled the abortion plans of the state's most powerful institution. What would He do for an encore? With
the Madison Surgery Center fight officially in the rearview
mirror, we needed to chart a new course for Vigil for Life.
Obviously, we'd continue hosting 40 Days for Life campaigns and prayer vigils throughout the year, but we wanted
to make sure that we continued to build upon the momentum created over the previous two years. If the pro-life community of Madison failed to take a step forward, it risked
taking two steps backward.

After batting about a number of ideas, the Vigil for
Life board of directors launched the "365 for Life Initiative"
whereby our volunteers would maintain a presence in front
of Planned Parenthood every day it was open, all year long.
The launch of the initiative became something of a commu-
nity-wide New Year's resolution as we began our vigil on
January 2, 2011. Since then, we've held vigil every business
day Planned Parenthood has been open.

Of course, our annual 40 Days for Life vigil remains Vigil for Life's flagship project. Shawn Carney flew to Madison to celebrate the Madison Surgery Center victory by speaking at our 2010 campaign kickoff event. And in 2011, Dr. Nancy Fredericks delivered the keynote speech at our opening rally. Dr. Fredericks said, "In our darkest days, when things looked bleak, and we didn't know how to press forward, my pro-life colleagues at the Madison Surgery Center and I would walk over to the window to watch you praying. It didn't matter whether it was cold, windy, rainy, or snowy; we knew you'd be there praying for us. And it gave us the strength to carry on."

In April of 2012, Dr. Fredericks received Pro-Life Wisconsin's "Angel of Life" award. Her revelation that our presence gave her and her colleagues strength encouraged us.

We've continued to host a twenty-four-hour vigil each fall. By the grace of God, not a single hour has gone uncovered.

Some of our volunteers took the momentum in a different direction. They noticed that the building across the street from Planned Parenthood was for sale. Three couples purchased it: Amy, who led Madison's 40 Days for Life campaign when we moved to town, and her husband, Tom; Greg, one of the Knights of Columbus men who inspired me by taking countless overnight hours at the 40 Days for Life vigil, and his wife, Ann; and Jeff and Sharon.

Amy noted that one of the significant dates in the property's acquisition was the Catholic feast day honoring Mary under the title "Our Lady of the Visitation." The three couples agreed to establish Our Lady of the Visitation, LLC, as the legal entity that would direct the building's future. "We agreed that was a great name," Greg said. "But in the process of doing the paperwork, I confused my Vs and named our partnership as Our Lady of Victory, LLC." Perhaps it was a mistake. I like to think it was the Holy Spirit at work, glorifying God for the victories He had won—and for the many victories still to come.

After a time of prayerful discernment, the owners renovated the building, and on January 17, 2012, established Wisconsin's second Women's Care Center location. The center now stands as a medical pregnancy help center, providing women facing crisis pregnancies with free ultrasounds, pregnancy testing, counseling, chastity education, post-abortion support, and more. Whereas Planned Parenthood sells more than eighty abortions for every adoption referral[1] (and according to former Planned Parenthood manager Sue Thayer, a referral often means just giving a woman a brochure about adoption), the Women's Care Center provides women in need of help with real alternatives, with real health care, and with real *choice*.

The year-round prayer and sidewalk counseling presence combined with a professional pregnancy help center across the street has led numerous women to turn away from Planned Parenthood and choose life. Meanwhile the state's abortion rate has dropped more than 27 percent, from 8,542 in 2009 to 6,224 in 2018.[2]

The abortion industry clearly felt the impact of our work. In January of 2014, then-Alderwoman Lisa Subeck— the same Lisa Subeck who, as executive director at NARAL Pro-Choice Wisconsin, described late-term abortions as "exciting"—introduced a buffer zone ordinance to effectively prohibit sidewalk counseling within city limits.[3] Having been elected to public office, Subeck was now using her newfound power to protect her own. "All patients going out to seek health care should be afforded the right to privacy and should be able to do it safely and freely and safe of intimidation and harassment," Subeck told NBC15 News in Madison.[4] Reporter Britni McDonald followed Subeck's remarks, adding, "[Subeck's] concern is the harassment of anti-abortion protesters."[5] McDonald's commentary was accompanied by video footage of an angry man shouting. As I watched the evening news piece, I recognized his face immediately. His shouting wasn't an example of "harassment of anti-abortion protesters." In fact, he was one of the pro-abortion agitators who—with Subeck—tried to disrupt our march to the Madison Surgery Center back in January of 2009. Subeck continued, "They can be very intimidating. They can really get into your personal space."[6]

Laura was invited to make the pro-life case against the buffer zone. Just as she had when she went head-to-head with the Planned Parenthood executive a few years earlier, she set the record straight:

> This is a crackdown on the right to free speech. . . . [Sidewalk counseling is] a peaceful opportunity to offer women an alternative in time of crisis. . . . They're free to come over and talk or continue in without even acknowledging our presence. We don't want our voice pushed out, which is what this . . . is trying to do.[7]

The City of Madison enacted Subeck's proposal, which was followed by a lawsuit from Vigil for Life participants and other pro-life leaders. The ordinance was never enforced, and, within months, the United States Supreme

Court struck down a similar ordinance in Boston. Shortly thereafter, Madison City Attorney Michael May officially announced that the city would not enforce the buffer zone.[8]

THE ROSARY GARDEN

On May 21, 2011, the late Bishop Robert Morlino dedicated the Miracle of Life Rosary Garden before a crowd of 350 people.[9] On the grounds of beautiful St. Mary Church in Pine Bluff, Wisconsin, the rosary garden is a brick pathway adorned with engraved bricks, flowers, and beautiful statues. Miscarried and stillborn babies are buried in the grassy center of the garden. The focal point is a life-sized statue of Mary holding the Christ child with a waterfall flowing down into a small pond. I was part of a small team of men who built the waterfall the previous year.

At the dedication, Fr. Heilman shared his vision. "The concept for this holy site came from much prayer and reflection," Fr. Richard Heilman said. "But, the first spark of inspiration came on the day we laid to rest little Gianna Karlen, the miscarried baby of Steve and Laura Karlen. While the place we had chosen for Gianna was nice, I realized we needed a place of great dignity, serenity, and prayer for these little ones and those who mourn their loss. From that day on, I became dedicated to this project, beginning with drawings I made using coffee can lids."[10]

Shortly after the dedication, Gianna was reinterred as the first child buried in the rosary garden. It's a beautiful and peaceful location, sandwiched between the little country church and cemetery. Behind the garden lies a cornfield. Altogether, the rosary garden provides a perfect place to reflect on the gift of life, the death we all will experience, and the hope of eternal life in heaven.

Not even a month after the dedication—on Father's Day, no less—Laura and I learned we were expecting once again. To become a father for the third time on Father's Day after years of infertility and a miscarriage felt like a plot right out of Hollywood. Each day that passed without trouble was a great gift. By the time we drove to our first sonogram appointment, we were already past the point in pregnancy where we miscarried Gianna. We were optimistic this meant that we had avoided whatever went wrong with our previous pregnancy and arose that morning with great joy and anticipation of meeting our child on the ultrasound screen. We finished a novena to St. Therese and excitedly bounded into the hospital for our appointment.

And that's where the similarities to Hollywood ended. Laura, Peter, and I should have seen the unmistakable flicker of a nascent heartbeat. Instead, the ultrasound showed us an image of a child who inexplicably quit growing several weeks earlier. We were completely devastated. How could this be happening again? This was supposed to be a happy day. This was the day we had waited years for.

I tried to come to terms with our new reality. Our first miscarriage was not an anomaly. I recalled a miscarriage memorial ceremony that Fr. Heilman held months earlier. One woman lit five candles representing the five babies she had lost. How many more would we lose? And was Peter destined to be an only child? We worked so hard to save the babies of complete strangers; how come we couldn't save our own?

I raised my head toward Laura, who continued to sob as she laid on the hospital bed. A sense of helplessness overcame me as I realized there was nothing in the world I could do to comfort my bride. And knowing that it was her polycystic ovarian syndrome that caused her miscarriages, Laura resented her own body as she struggled to shake a sense of guilt that she was to blame.

"Do you wish you had married someone who could carry children to term?" she sometimes asked me. The question always broke my heart. In a way our struggle with infertility and recurrent miscarriage was a mirror image of the helplessness I experienced on the sidewalk in front of Planned Parenthood. Out on the streets, I was forced to accept that I was powerless to prevent a woman from ending the life of her child in the womb. Here in the cold, dark ultrasound room, I realized I was powerless to help my wife sustain the life of our child. The person I loved the most was in pain, and there was nothing I could do about it. We composed ourselves to the best of our abilities and went home, heartbroken, to await the delivery of another miscarried child.

After a day at home picking up the pieces of our shattered dreams, I had to go back to work. I was lucky to have an office to myself because I spent the first half day back on the job staring blankly at the wall with tears in my eyes. I was blessed with colleagues who understood and appreciated our struggle. Other people weren't as sensitive.

"How far along was your wife when she miscarried?"

"Not that far—only the second month."

"Oh, so that's not that bad then. It would be a lot worse if this happened later in the pregnancy."

Even among many pro-lifers, there seemed to be an implicit assumption that a baby lost early in pregnancy wasn't nearly as valuable as a baby lost later. Certainly, the loss of a child later in pregnancy can have emotional implications that involve greater degrees of suffering, but I wasn't willing to concede that our losses were insignificant either.

A month after our fateful ultrasound, Laura still had not delivered the body. It was a miserable month. We prayed that perhaps God would hear our desperate pleas and revive the baby with a miracle. Eventually, since my wife still appeared to be pregnant, our doctor suggested maybe the ultrasound tech had made a mistake. But that glimmer of hope merely provided an additional opportunity for our dreams to be crushed when the initial diagnosis was confirmed.

In the weeks to come, my wife's emotional agony was compounded by tremendous physical pain. Together we grieved deeply. On one hand, it was difficult to want the miscarriage to complete. Laura simply didn't want to relinquish the child within her. On the other hand, I yearned for closure. I wanted to begin the process of moving on. I mourned the loss of our child, certainly, but not in quite the way a mother does.

For the rest of the summer, Laura never quite seemed herself. Whether it was a family trip to the zoo, a get-together with friends, or a lazy weekend at home, the pain of losing her precious child never left her face. I'll forever remember the summer of 2011 as the summer when my wife didn't smile. As summer turned to fall, I began to wonder whether I would ever see her smile again.

TAKE ME OUT TO THE BALLGAME

The one thing that provided joy in our lives was, perhaps, the most trivial thing of all: my beloved Milwaukee Brewers. After a couple of down years, the Brewers hit the 2011 season with a retooled pitching staff and were ready to take the league by storm. After a slow start, the Brewers picked up steam. They saved their best for the worst month of our lives. Weighed down by sorrow, we needed them to win to give us something, *anything* to be happy about. And nearly every day they did. Wild wins and incredible comebacks became a daily occurrence.

By the end of the regular season, the Brewers were division champs, finishing with a team record ninety-six wins. I had attended eight games in Milwaukee. When the Brewers held a fan pep rally prior to the playoffs, I took the day off of work to bring Peter, then four years old, to the celebration. But before we got in the car to head to Milwaukee, I logged in at my favorite team blog and pounded out a hastily written article describing just what the season meant to me.

> I told my wife last night that I suspect a guy's favorite season of baseball should take place when he's 10 or 12 years old rather than 27. But regardless of how this season ends—with a World Series title, an ugly sweep or anything in between—I had more fun this year than I ever have watching baseball.

I recounted the sorrow brought upon our family by the miscarriage and how the Brewers hot streak provided a welcome distraction during our darkest days. The full blog post included more "inside baseball" than is worth mentioning here, but I closed the post describing just why a children's game brought me so much joy.

> As I rode the escalator down from the cheap seats (at my all-time high 8th game of the year!) last night, my wife asked me if I had a good

time. I couldn't answer her. I knew I'd get emotional . . . about a baseball game.

But it was more than that. And it was more than a much-needed escape. You see, the Brewers became the first real shared hobby that my four-year-old and I could bond over. He sat through six games, absolutely absorbed to the last pitch. He'll point out Ryan Braun or Rickie Weeks in the on-deck circle from row 15 of the Terrace Reserved cheap seats. And each day, the first words out of his mouth are "Daddy, did the Brewers win? Can we watch the headlights?" Ha! I'm still sad about the two children I've lost, but baseball has given me an awesome tool for cementing my father-son relationship with the little man that we do have. For that I will always be grateful.

I didn't expect anybody to read it. Fan submissions are tucked into a sidebar of the website and rarely get much attention. That was ok. I wasn't writing for an audience; I was writing for catharsis.

Before long, I learned I was writing for both. Encouraging feedback came in fast and furious. Other fans shared their condolences or even opened up about their own experiences losing a child. Within hours, blog moderators bumped my hidden sidebar article to a front-page featured story. And the very next day, I got a call from one of Milwaukee's television network affiliates. A producer had read my post, and he wanted to do a segment about it. Laura, Peter, and I rushed to the ballpark one more time.

The piece provided a great covert opportunity to witness to the sanctity of life. We didn't need to talk about abortion.

That meant viewers didn't put up their guard or fall back on slogans and talking points. Our grief and our love for the babies we had lost said more than enough about the dignity of the pre-born child.

MIDNIGHT AT THE EMERGENCY ROOM

By the time Laura finally went into labor to complete the miscarriage, there were complications. She began hemorrhaging. Dr. Kloess told us we needed to get to the emergency room. Even though it was already after 10:00 p.m., our friends Andrew and Laura Forecki rushed over to our apartment. Laura Forecki spent the night with Peter, and Andrew agreed to drive us to the hospital so I could tend to my wife in the backseat.

These are the moments no bride and groom ever spend their wedding day thinking about. But this evening, as awful as it was, was the fulfillment of the promises we made the day we got married. As I carried my fading wife to the car because she lacked the strength to get there on her own, a strange realization came over me: I was completely at peace. This was the worst night of my life. But amidst the agony, God's grace made me thankful for the opportunity not only to care for but also to share in the sufferings of the person in this world I love the most.

When we arrived at the emergency room, Laura was in terrible physical pain and even worse emotional pain. Still, she couldn't resist bearing pro-life witness to the medical personnel who attended to her. When one of the providers spoke with her about passing the "products of conception," Laura used what little strength she had left to remind him that this was her baby he was talking about.

We named our child Gerard after the patron saint of mothers. Once again, our relatives and our pro-life family came through for us. In August, we were joined by both to bury Gerard only a few feet away from his sister in the Miracle of Life Rosary Garden. And again, we hadn't even met some of our guests prior to the burial, but moved by our loss, their Christian charity prompted them to get in the car, drive to south-central Wisconsin, and spend their evening attending the burial of a miscarried child whose parents they didn't know.

Just before miscarrying, Laura read a book that reminded us that sometimes God allows people to suffer as a means of preparing them to serve others undergoing suffering. That certainly proved to be the case with us. In the weeks that followed, I received a call from a Milwaukee-area resident.

"You don't know me," the voice on the other end of the line said. "But I heard you have a sacred place where miscarried babies can be buried with respect and dignity." The woman who was calling me had lost *three* children to miscarriage. But without anywhere appropriate to lay them to rest, she held on to their remains until something suitable emerged. "I know that might sound weird," she said, "but I won't just bury them in the yard like a dog." I gave her Fr. Heilman's direct line, and shortly thereafter she was able to bury her children. Her three babies are now the only three in the rosary garden who pre-date our Gianna.

Laura, too, received a call from a woman whose daughter was miscarrying. The opportunity to share in their grief was powerful for both Laura and the family, who also buried the child in the rosary garden. Years later, word has spread, and one Madison hospital even refers miscarrying parents out to tiny Pine Bluff, Wisconsin. The Lord visibly fulfilled

Romans 8:28, the Scripture verse we chose for Gerard's tombstone: "We know that all things work for good for those who love God."

While we were blessed by the rosary garden, the opportunity to aid in the healing of others who lost children to miscarriage, and the support of our family and friends, the pain of our loss lingered. The Lord had used us to save the lives of so many other pre-born babies, but we couldn't manage to bring our own safely into the world. For the first time, we began to seriously consider the possibility that the Lord wouldn't bless us with another living child. That notion seemed inconceivable four and a half years earlier when Peter was born only ten months into our marriage.

Maybe it was the lush cornfields of Pine Bluff or my affinity for baseball that led me to reflect on a scene from the modern-classic film *Field of Dreams*. Played by Burt Lancaster, the ghost of former professional baseball player "Moonlight" Graham recounts the story of his one day in the big leagues. He played a mere inning in the field, never receiving the chance to bat. He never spent another day in the majors. "You know we just don't recognize the most significant moments of our lives while they're happening," Graham says. "Back then, I thought, 'Well, there'll be other days. I didn't realize that that was the *only* day.'"[11] The day Peter was born, I thought there would be other days. Perhaps April 16, 2007, was the only day.

The pain of the two miscarriages in fifteen months led Laura and me to seek a change of scenery. There was too much pain in our two-bedroom apartment. We needed to get out, so we bought our first home.

Laura was so proud to have a place of our own. For the first time in months, she seemed happy—even if scars remained. As we unpacked in our new home, I distinctly remember stuffing bins of baby toys, clothes, and supplies into the attic, cynically thinking, *Well, we'll never need this stuff again.* But, once more, the Lord wasn't done with us yet.

18

Full Circle

〜〜〜

A couple of days before Christmas, we visited La Crosse, Wisconsin, a few hours away from Madison, so I could lead a caroling event in front of the abortion referral center in town. The area is home for Cardinal Raymond Burke, who—as bishop of La Crosse—established the Shrine of Our Lady of Guadalupe. It's a beautiful church and campus dedicated to the Mother of God as she appeared to a humble Aztec peasant in 1531, ultimately paving the way for the conversion of Mexico to Christianity and an end to the barbaric Aztec practice of human sacrifice. That's why Our Lady of Guadalupe is known to Catholics as the patroness of both the Americas and of pre-born children.

Prior to our visit, a friend shared with me that the shrine held gloves that belonged to St. Gianna. Because St. Gianna heroically laid down her own life to save that of her pre-born child, God has been known to work through St. Gianna's relics to answer the prayers of infertile couples. My friend told me that if we'd like, he'd be happy to arrange some time for us to venerate the gloves while we were in town. It took us about two seconds to accept the offer.

When we arrived at the shrine, we were guided to a private room and presented with a box containing the gloves. Laura asked whether there was anything we should know about venerating the gloves. I knew my wife well enough to know *exactly* what she was up to. When the shrine employee simply encouraged us to spend as much time as we'd like in prayer and stepped out of the room, Laura didn't waste a second in putting the gloves on.

"Laura, do you think you're supposed to do that?"

"I asked her what we should know about venerating the gloves," my wife responded. "She didn't say *not* to."

The gloves fit Laura's hands perfectly. That was quite unexpected given that Laura is rather petite at less than five feet tall. For the next twenty minutes, we prayed fervently, asking that if it was the Lord's will, we'd be blessed with another living child. At the time, Laura had been on fertility medication prescribed by Dr. Kloess, but, as we left the shrine, I made a proposal: "Laura, if we're going to ask the Lord and Our Lady and St. Gianna for a miracle today, maybe we should put our money where our mouth is and go off the meds. He doesn't need those pills to answer our prayers."

Laura agreed. Two weeks later, she was pregnant.

The pregnancy wasn't easy. Dr. Kloess believed the cause of her miscarriages was a deficiency in progesterone, the hormone that sustains babies during pregnancy. So twice a week, I'd give Laura two shots of a progesterone oil so thick it took several minutes to inject. Generally, I did a good job. Thankfully, Laura has forgiven me for the night I missed the spot and put a sharp needle right into her sciatic nerve. (Don't worry; she regained feeling in her legs by morning.) It didn't matter what was going on or how late we were up, we had to do those injections. And every two weeks, Laura headed to the hospital for a blood draw to check her levels.

Once again, we couldn't escape a connection with abortion. The progesterone deficiency endangered our babies in the same way the abortion pill regimen—a progesterone blocker—endangers babies. And the progesterone supplementation we provided Laura was the same type of treatment used as an antidote when mothers who take abortion pills change their mind and attempt to reverse their abortions.

HOPES, FEARS, AND ULTRASOUND

Come February, things were not looking good. Over the course of a month, her progesterone levels had steadily dropped. By all indications, our baby had died, Laura's body quit making its own progesterone, and only our injections were keeping her from completing the miscarriage. Dr. Kloess referred us for an ultrasound.

As we drove to our appointment, we prayed and we braced ourselves for confirmation of our worst fears. By this point, the mere sight of the ultrasound room sent chills down my spine. *What a bizarre reaction!* I thought. After all, the ultrasound machine—by illustrating the humanity of unborn children—is the world's most effective tool available for saving lives from abortion. When they meet their babies via the ultrasound machine, countless abortion-vulnerable mothers fall in love and are moved to choose life.

But for us, the cold, dark ultrasound room had been a place where our dreams went to die. As our appointment began, Laura gripped my hand. The ultrasound technician said she'd begin with the less invasive abdominal ultrasound, but that if Laura wasn't far enough along, she'd have to move along to a more invasive vaginal ultrasound.

It wasn't necessary. Only a moment after applying the ultrasound probe, we saw a clear and healthy heartbeat. Laura recognized it right away and began crying tears of joy. I was too stunned to know what to say. And Peter, who came with us because we didn't have time to arrange a baby-sitter, simply said, "Congratulations, Mommy and Daddy!" Our family's joy brought the ultrasound technician herself to tears.

The rest of the pregnancy was rocky, with early contractions and progesterone levels all over the map, but on October 3, 2012, John Paul Charles Karlen arrived safely into the world. We named our son after St. Pope John Paul II, who had lived through both the Nazi occupation and Soviet occupation of Poland, all while managing to keep a smile on his face—and the joy of the gospel in his heart.

The same pro-life community that helped us mourn the losses of Gianna and Gerard came out to celebrate John Paul's baptism. Fr. Mark, who helped me dig Gianna's grave two and a half years earlier, drove down to perform the sacrament while Jen Dunnett, a friend we first met through 40 Days for Life, agreed to be John Paul's godmother. Close to two hundred people flooded our tiny church for a standing-room-only Mass.

FROM MADISON TO MEXICO

Within three weeks of John Paul's birth, I stepped down from my position at Pro-Life Wisconsin. It had been a tremendous experience. Not only did we train sidewalk counselors across Wisconsin, but we also helped launch new 40 Days for Life campaigns around the state. My tenure also coincided with a series of legislative victories, including the closing of a legal loophole designed to prevent the University of Wisconsin or its affiliated hospital and clinics from revisiting the idea of opening an abortion center.

I loved my work with Pro-Life Wisconsin and particularly relished the opportunity to work alongside my friend and mentor Matt Sande. From advocacy to education to public policy, we had built a movement. But when I received an opportunity to join the 40 Days for Life staff, I couldn't resist. On October 22, 2012, I became the director of North American outreach for 40 Days for Life. Everything had come full circle. My first pro-life activity was volunteering for 40 Days for Life. I helped launch new campaigns at Pro-Life Wisconsin. And now—exactly five years after stress and frustration led me to exclaim to Laura, "I wish I had never even heard of 40 Days for Life; I hate 40 Days for Life!"— I was on the 40 Days for Life headquarters team.

As unlikely as it might seem, it was those moments of persevering through the temptation to despair that equipped me for the job. From the outside, it would be easy to conclude that 40 Days for Life is an unstoppable baby-saving force. The local leaders know otherwise. They know every victory comes only after tremendous sacrifice. In Madison, we endured many setbacks, disappointments, and broken hearts without the guarantee of success. We proceeded despite personal failings, occasional infighting, and inexperience.

After the Madison Surgery Center's abortion plan was scrapped, we could see how God used every last trial to weave together a historic victory. But in those difficult moments, we had nothing to go on but faith. In my new role with 40 Days for Life, I'd be able to draw on my own experience to encourage leaders to keep going, even when things look bleakest.

The morning I reluctantly joined my first pro-life vigil, I didn't set out to one day work full time in the pro-life movement. I just wanted to help save even one woman like Laura's friend Jessica from making the worst decision of her life. God has now used that desire across the continent as my work with 40 Days for Life has brought me to more than two hundred campaigns; I've addressed pro-lifers in all fifty states, four Canadian provinces, and Mexico City.

My visit to Mexico City's campaigns ranks among the most memorable. After spending two days visiting abortion facilities and pro-life leaders across the city, we arrived at the Marie Stopes abortion center at five o'clock in the morning on day 40 of the 2015 spring campaign. I initially assumed the early start time was a typo. Laura, who accompanied me as my interpreter, and I took a deep breath when we realized it wasn't. As the sun rose, pro-lifers from all over the city converged and began decorating their cars with the blue and white 40 Days for Life colors. Eventually, a bus showed up and was outfitted with 40 Days for Life banners.

Laura and I were scheduled to ride with Lourdes, the pro-life leader who brought 40 Days for Life to Mexico, but I couldn't refuse an opportunity to ride the 40 Days for Life bus leading a caravan to the Basilica of Our Lady of Guadalupe. For the entire ride, the pro-life prayer warriors prayed, sang hymns, waved pom poms, and shouted "¡Gloria a Dios!" (Glory to God!)

Our arrival to the basilica was unforgettable. This was the site where the mother of Jesus appeared nearly five hundred years ago, converting the people, setting the country on fire for Christ, and ending child sacrifice in Mexico. Palm Sunday Mass doubled as the closing Mass for the Lenten 40 Days for Life campaign. After Mass, we marched over to an auditorium. With Laura translating for me, I spoke to both the media and hundreds of 40 Days for Life volunteers representing three Mexico City vigils to close that spring's campaign.

The day provided an unforgettable cultural and faith-filled experience, but for Laura and me, it carried even deeper significance: just a few months earlier, on the Feast of Our Lady of Guadalupe, we learned we were expecting once again.

The pregnancy had once again been rocky, involving another hospital visit for an ultrasound that we fully expected would confirm fears of a third miscarriage. But, at nearly twenty weeks along, Laura, baby, and I were on a pro-life pilgrimage of a lifetime. When we returned to Mexico City three months later to host a sidewalk counseling workshop, we made time for another side visit to the basilica. And on August 17, Teresa *Guadalupe* Karlen was born. Dr. Kloess, who had done so much to keep Teresa alive while she was in utero, and his wife, Laura, agreed to be her godparents.

While our daughter's middle name is a tribute to the patroness of both the Americas and the pro-life movement, her first name is in homage to St. Mother Teresa of Calcutta. One of the great saints of the twentieth century, Mother Teresa lived in abject poverty, bringing love to lepers and AIDS victims dying in the slums of her filthy city. While there are certainly many differences between her work and ours in the streets of Madison, we also found a number of similarities. The men and women Mother Teresa served in her Home for the Dying were often people whose spiritual poverty matched their material poverty. Her work took her into great darkness—a darkness she was willing to accept out of her love for the Lord. Mother Teresa wrote to her spiritual director, "For the first time . . . I have come to love the darkness—for I believe now that it is a part, a very, very small part of Jesus' darkness and pain on earth."[1]

When a foreigner inspired by Mother Teresa's work heroically offered to leave behind all comfort, security, and affluence and join her in the slums of Calcutta, India, Mother Teresa's response was as shocking as it was instructive:

> "Stay where you are. Find your own Calcutta. Find the sick, the suffering, and the lonely, right where you are—in your own homes and in your own families . . . in your workplaces and in your schools. You can find Calcutta all over the world, if you have eyes to see. Everywhere, wherever you go, you find people who are unwanted, unloved, uncared for, just rejected by society—completely forgotten, completely left alone."[2]

While the women we strive to serve where we live might not be as materially destitute as those Mother Teresa served in India, the spiritual poverty and darkness that lead a woman to end the life of her own child are every bit as tragic. Mother Teresa's example of entering into that darkness to love our neighbor without counting the cost made her a more-than-worthy namesake for our new daughter.

OUR LORD PROVIDES THROUGH OUR LADY

As the day of Teresa's birth came to a close, I left the hospital to go home for the night. When I got in my car, I realized that our baby's connection to Our Lady of Guadalupe wasn't her only connection to the mother of God.

A year earlier, a generous friend took us to France. The highlight of the trip was a pilgrimage to Lourdes, where Mary appeared to a young peasant girl named Bernadette. Since the apparition, the natural spring at the site has been associated with many miraculous healings. The waters are accessible to all, and there are even opportunities to bathe privately in the water. Seeking healing from the polycystic ovarian syndrome that made pregnancy so difficult to achieve and sustain, Laura had her heart set on bathing in the healing waters of Lourdes. Unfortunately, we arrived late and *just* missed the window of opportunity. We had to leave before the baths would re-open. Laura, longing to be cured, cried, but our friend reminded us that, although the Lord often uses the water to confer healing, He doesn't *need* it.

We spent the night in Lourdes and planned to leave the following morning. As we prepared to board our van, a few members of our group were still getting ready. The rest of us browsed the gift shops across the street from our hotel. Before long we realized we couldn't find Laura. She didn't have her phone, and our group began frantically searching for her. Still longing for healing, Laura ran down the street to the apparition site to anoint herself with the healing water and to pray one last time for a miracle.

It wasn't my finest moment as a husband, but when we found her, I scolded my wife. How could she run off like that? Wasn't she concerned about being rude to the friend who took us all the way to France? Did she know how worried we were? I was fuming! Though I was upset, Laura got the last laugh in the end. After two C-sections, we knew we'd have to schedule a C-section for Teresa's birth. We desired August 14, the Feast of St. Maximilian Kolbe. The hospital insisted on August 17. It wasn't until I got in the car to drive home from the hospital after my daughter's birth that evening that I realized Teresa was born a year to the day from Laura's rogue escapade in Lourdes.

In November of 2014—the month before we learned Teresa Guadalupe was on the way—I called Sister Cecile, a religious sister who led numerous 40 Days for Life campaigns in the Canadian province of New Brunswick. I wanted to inquire about how her campaign went. When Sister Cecile asked about my family, I told her I was married and had two boys.

"You need some girls!" she replied.

"Well, you'll have to talk to the Lord about that," I answered. "We'd like more children, but it doesn't come easily for us."

"I'll do that. You'll have two girls."

Just nine months later, we were halfway there. But not quite a year and a half after that—on the Feast of Our Lady of Lourdes, to be exact—Laura took another positive pregnancy test. Once again, after another challenging pregnancy, daughter number two arrived on October 13, 2017. Again, knowing she'd need a C-section, Laura chose to deliver on the anniversary of the Miracle of the Sun—the great sign exhibited by Our Lady of Fatima, which was witnessed by 70,000 people[3] as a sign of the authenticity of her apparitions to three peasant children in Portugal.

Though she was born on the feast day of Our Lady of Fatima, Katherine Lourdes is named after Catherine of Siena, the patron saint of miscarriage whom we count on to see us through each pregnancy, and, of course, Our Lady of Lourdes.

I don't know whether Sister Cecile was just sharing her wishes for me the day she forecasted we'd have two daughters or if she had a direct line to God. But as I gaze upon my daughters—both of whom we learned about on great Marian feast days—I can't help but to suspect it's the latter.

Postscript

∿

More than a decade has passed since Jessica had her abortion. Though I never actually had the opportunity to meet Jessica, I think about her often. Her abortion still pains me. Her grief-ridden phone call to Laura breaking the news of her abortion is still my greatest motivator and most salient reminder of why we take the time to pray in front of abortion facilities. When I speak, audience members sometimes ask me where she is now and how she's doing. I ask those questions too—and many more.

What is she up to now?

Has she found healing?

Is she at peace?

I don't know. I may never know. But I believe we have great reason to hope because our God is a God of transformation. I've seen that firsthand. After all, it's our God of transformation who turned my pro-choice wife into a steadfast pro-life advocate in a matter of minutes. It's our God who moved me to sacrifice Green Bay Packer Sundays to pray at the vigil site. It's our God who toppled plans for a late-term abortion center in one of the most abortion-friendly cities in the nation. It's our God who plucked a down-and-out twenty-five-year-old and used him to spread the Gospel of Life in Honolulu, Anchorage, Montreal, Mexico City, and everywhere in between. And it's our God of transformation who has blessed an infertile couple with five adorable children—Benedict Michael Karlen was born on December 9, 2019—restoring to my wife's face the smile I once feared I would never see again.

"Love one another," Jesus tells us. The command sounds simple, and it is. But in Madison, Wisconsin, simple acts of love built community, ended late-term abortion, and helped heal the broken hearts suffered by my wife and me in the wake of losing two children to miscarriage.

I found myself dramatically outnumbered in one of America's most socially liberal cities, but folks like Jeanne Breunig, Adam Morse, Matt Sande, Fr. Rick Heilman, my wife Laura, and so many others saw a threat to their community and dared to believe their prayers would be heard and answered. Amy (Hying) Lang spent countless hours huddled around a spreadsheet, begging people to sign up to come out to her 40 Days for Life vigil. And, with little hope of success, Dr. Nancy Fredericks put her job and her livelihood on the line to stand up for what's right.

As a result, there is no late-term abortion center in Madison, Wisconsin—at the University of Wisconsin or anywhere else.

Dr. Michael and Laura Kloess saw the often-overlooked dignity of the poor and uninsured in their community and stood up to declare that authentic health care means a practice that doesn't contradict the Hippocratic Oath by providing or referring for abortion, contraception, sterilization, or euthanasia. They made tremendous sacrifices to establish Our Lady of Hope Clinic, providing Madison with one of the country's most unique medical practices—a practice that provides two-thirds of its appointments to uninsured residents and demolishes the myth that social justice advocates need to make a choice between caring for the poor or for pre-born children.

Fr. Rick Heilman and Fr. Mark Vander Steeg recognized that an authentic culture of life requires respect not only for pre-born babies lost to abortion but also for those lost to miscarriage. Because of their vision, parents who have lost children before birth have come from around the state to bury and to honor their miscarried and stillborn children in Pine Bluff and Greenville, Wisconsin.

Greg and Ann Wagner, Tom and Amy Lang, and Jeff and Sharon Davis invested their finances and countless hours to establish the Women's Care Center so that no expectant mother is driven to an abortion decision out of a lack of support from the community.

None of these individuals across Wisconsin set out to be heroes. To quote Catholic author Michael O'Brien, they simply "[gave] life in a season of death and were willing to pay the price." Seeing a need in their community and— moved by their love for both God and neighbor—they set out to fill that need. Even when it was difficult. Even when it was boring. Even when it put a strain on their time and their finances.

St. Catherine of Siena has been quoted as saying, "Be who God meant you to be and you will set the world ablaze." Ordinary women and men in Madison, Wisconsin, answered the Lord's call and set their community ablaze for God, ablaze for life.

In doing so, they proved that being authentically pro-life is as simple as loving, especially when it hurts the most to love. And that takes me back, full circle to January of 2007. The same month that Laura's friend Jessica had her abortion I saw firsthand what it means to "love one another."

Another couple we knew from our time at the University of Wisconsin had moved to Chicago following graduation. The man's dad had terminal cancer, and when it became clear that his remaining days were few, Laura and I drove across town to spend an evening with the family. We hoped to simply visit, help out around the house, and try to be good friends.

Shortly after dinner, the father—who had been resting—was going to come meet us. He'd had an upset stomach, and on his way up, he was unable to make it to the bathroom. He'd had an accident. He had soiled himself. It was an uncomfortable moment to say the least. Personally, I was disgusted. I was embarrassed for this man. I wished I could teleport myself to anywhere other than where I was. And I'm ashamed to admit that the words that immediately went through my mind were something to the effect of, *My God! This man has no dignity!*

But what happened next changed everything. The man's wife, who had been patiently caring for him during a long and painful decline, rushed over to his side. She sweetly spoke words of comfort to him. She smiled at him, kissed him on the cheek, and wheeled him away to the restroom to clean him up.

I chastised myself immediately. This man was in his final days. Cancer and chemo had ravaged his body to the point that he looked like a Picasso painting. He was confined to a wheelchair, and he'd just soiled himself in front of a house full of guests. Yet, his wife's tender care made him the most dignified man in the world.

Such is the paradox. This moment was wretched and painful, but it was also the purest and truest expression of love I've ever seen. It was something that no spouse ever wants to go through, but it was the absolute pinnacle of human love. This moment was the closest I've ever seen human love mirror the love of Almighty God.

The great British writer G. K. Chesterton calls this the "great lesson of Beauty and the Beast; that a thing must be loved BEFORE it is loveable."[1]

So, too, it is with all human life: The child with spina bifida. The child who will certainly die within a day of birth. My little friend with Down syndrome. Their value is not reduced by their disabilities. They are only unwanted so long as we *choose* not to want them. They are only unloved as long as we *choose* not to love them.

You don't need to spend much time in front of an abortion facility to meet women facing desperate circumstances. On any given day you might meet a teenager, terrified to come home and tell Mom and Dad that she's pregnant. Or perhaps a couple who received a devastating prenatal diagnosis and is being tempted or even pressured into having an abortion. You might meet a woman who is the victim of an assault—and became pregnant through that assault. These are difficult situations, and I won't pretend that any of them have an easy answer.

But what I can say with absolute certainty is that when we as a society encounter a woman in crisis and tell her, "I'm sorry but the best we can do for you—the best we're willing to do for you—is to take your money and kill your baby," that's not good enough. That sends a message, not just to that woman but to the entire world, that there's not enough love in our hearts or in God's heart to help her triumph over a desperate situation. It sends a message that there is no hope. Abortion is a product of despair.

But in the example of our Lord, who walked before us, we find great reason for hope, and we learn how we are to respond to the tragedy of abortion. In His ministry on earth, our Lord entered into some of the most miserable situations the human experience has to offer: leprosy, prostitution, the abuse of widows and orphans, the stoning of sinners, a brutally oppressive government—I could go on and on. But our Lord entered into and even shared in the sufferings of His people.

And He calls us to do the same.

That's why we do crazy things like pray in front of abortion facilities, start new pregnancy help centers, and dig the graves of miscarried children who would otherwise never be remembered: to bear the light of Christ, shining in the darkness.

Acknowledgments

~~~

First and foremost, I give thanks to God Almighty for the gift of life, for the hope of eternal life through the death and resurrection of His only begotten Son, Jesus Christ, and for the opportunity to play some small part in building a culture of life.

I am grateful to my parents, Chuck and Debbie. Dad's example of hard work, integrity, and refusal to make excuses sets a standard I strive to live by. Mom's passion and commitment to always doing what's right kept me fighting against long odds.

This book would not exist without Shawn Carney, whose mentorship, friendship, and encouragement made it possible.

The heroic sacrifices made by Matt and Rebecca Sande; Tom and Amy Lang; Jen Dunnett; David Stiennon; Greg and Ann Wagner; Ron Faust; Dave and Jill Yanke; Matt Bowman; Curt Jacobsen; Will Goodman; Jeanne Breunig; Del, Terri, Buck, and Andy Teeter; Dr. John Bohn; Adam Morse; Alissa Hirscher; and Dr. Nancy Fredericks continue to inspire me, and I could not be more grateful for their fellowship and friendship.

Dr. Michael and Laura Kloess are living saints.

I thank God for the gift of faithful and holy clergy, especially Fr. Mark Vander Steeg, Fr. Rick Heilman, Fr. Jorge Miramontes, Fr. Chris Gernetzke, Monsignor Mike Burke, Fr. David Greenfield, Bishop Donald Hying, Bishop Thomas Olmsted, Cardinal Raymond Burke, Deacon Chris Schmelzer (and his wife Patti), Deacon Dave DeYoung, Deacon David Delaney, and the late Bishop Robert Morlino, who continue to point us toward heaven.

I am particularly grateful for the countless anonymous prayer warriors who sacrificed their time in freezing cold, pouring rain, and vitriolic insults to stand in front of the Madison Surgery Center and Planned Parenthood, daring to believe their prayers would be heard and answered.

It's a tremendous blessing to take the field of spiritual battle with my talented and selfless 40 Days for Life colleagues: Robert Colquhoun, Sue Thayer, Dr. Haywood Robinson, Lourdes Varela, Melinda Giambo, Bobby Reynoso, Dawn Crawford, Tommy Tellson, Gilbert Gonzales, Jill Copeland, Ben Starnes, and Cheryl Tamez—especially Dr. Robinson, who ventured into a blustery Wisconsin winter to stand with us. Board members Matt Britton, Carol Siedhoff, Segundo de los Heros Monereo, Alfonso Chicharro, John Barnett, and Fr. Paul Felix generously give their time and talent to serve the least of our brothers and sisters.

Thank you to Dr. Carrie Gress, my editor, whose encouragement and feedback spurred this project forward.

I am grateful for the constant love and support from my in-laws, Joe and Jean.

And finally, thank you to my family. Peter, John Paul, Teresa, Katherine, and Benedict, it's a gift to be the dad of such loving, sweet, and hilarious kids.

Last but not least, Laura, life with you is the grandest of adventures. I love you and can't wait to see what God has in store for us next.

Notes

CHAPTER 1

1. "Abortion and Mental Health Risks," AfterAbortion.org, https://afterabortion.org/abortion-risks-a-list-of-major-psycho logical-complications-related-to-abortion/ (author name and date unavailable).

2. Ibid.

CHAPTER 2

1. "Madison mayor's proposed motto: '77 Square Miles Surrounded by Reality,'" *Milwaukee Journal Sentinel*, July 12, 2013, http://archive.jsonline.com/news/wisconsin/madison-mayors-pro posed-motto-77-square-miles-surrounded-by-reality-b9953046z1 -215234061.html/ (author name unavailable).

2. Jim VandeHei, "The Boss Makes a Pitch for Kerry," *Washington Post*, October 29, 2004, http://www.washingtonpost.com/wp-dyn/ articles/A7421-2004Oct28.html.

CHAPTER 3

1. Staff, "League Vows to Fight New Planned Parenthood Facility," Pro-Life Action League, July 27, 2007, http://prolifeaction. org/hotline/2007/ppaurora/.

2. David Bereit and Shawn Carney, *40 Days for Life* (Nashville, TN: Cappella Books, 2017).

3. Ibid.

4. https://www.40daysforlife.com/about-overview.aspx.

5. Staff, "40-Day Vigil Launched to Halt 'Abortion Fortress,'" Pro-Life Action League, August 14, 2007, http://prolifeaction.org/hotline/2007/ppaurora2/.

6. Steven Ertelt, "Michael Clancy: The Photographer Whose Amazing Pro-Life Picture Changed the World," LifeNews.com, July 4, 2008, http://www.lifenews.com/2008/07/04/nat-4018/.

7. Michael Clancy, "Hand of Hope: The Story Behind the Picture," http://michaelclancy.com/?page_id=94.

8. Ibid.

9. Robert Davis, "Fetus 'hand' photo stirs abortion evidence debate," *The Californian*, May 3, 2000; https://www.newspapers.com/image/515635540/.

CHAPTER 4

1. *Amazing Grace*, Steven Knight, writer; Michael Apted, director (2007).

CHAPTER 5

1. Emily Sorensen, "PowPAC's 'Making God Laugh' opens Friday," *San Diego Tribune*, November 8, 2017, https://www.sandiego uniontribune.com/pomerado-news/entertainment/sd-cm-pow-ent-making-god-laugh-20171108-story.html.

2. Pioneer Press, "UW says it won't profit from late-term abortions," *St. Paul Pioneer Press*, January 29, 2009, https://www.twin cities.com/2009/01/29/uw-says-it-wont-profit-from-late-term-abortions/.

3. Alliance Defending Freedom, https://web.archive.org/web/20191110090247/http://adflegal.org/detailspages/faith-and-justice-details/the-lifeguard (originally accessed as "The Lifeguard," cover story, *Faith & Justice* 4:2, July 1, 2011, http://adflegal.org/detailspages/faith-and-justice-details/the-lifeguard).

4. Ibid.

5. "'Secret' University of Wisconsin plans for mid-term abortion clinic revealed," Catholic News Agency, January 7, 2009, http://www.catholicnewsagency.com/news/secret_university_of_wisconsin_plans_for_midterm_abortion_clinic_revealed/.

6. Angelina Baglini, JD, "Gestational Limits on Abortion in the United States Compared to International Norms," Charlotte

Lozier Institute, February 1, 2014, http://www.lozierinstitute.org/internationalabortionnorms/.

7. Rich Lowry, "Obama the abortion extremist," Politico.com, August 23, 2012, https://www.politico.com/story/2012/08/the-abortion-extremist-080013.

8. Peter Kirsanow, "Clarifying Obama's Vote on Born-Alive," *National Review*, February 10, 2012, http://www.nationalreview.com/corner/290764/clarifying-obamas-vote-born-alive-peter-kirsanow.

9. Born-Alive Infants Protection Act of 2002, H.R. 2175, 107th Cong. (2002), https://www.congress.gov/bill/107th-congress/house-bill/2175.

10. Michael Baggot, "Obama Declares He Doesn't Want His Children 'Punished with a Baby,'" LifeSiteNews.com, April 1, 2008, https://www.lifesitenews.com/news/obama-declares-he-doesnt-want-his-children-punished-with-a-baby.

11. Michãˆ Le Marr, "Soul Food," *Los Angeles Times*, February 18, 2009, https://www.latimes.com/socal/daily-pilot/news/tn-dpt-xpm-2009-02-18-hbi-soulfood02192009-story.html.

CHAPTER 6

1. David Wahlberg, "Abortion Clinic is Proposed\The UW-Meriter Facility Would Mainly Offer Second-Trimester Abortions," Madison.com, January 7, 2009, https://madison.com/news/abortion-clinic-is-proposed-the-uw-meriter-facililty-would-mainly/article_b65ab85d-5a37-5464-a2b3-25cb05678ceb.html.

2. Ibid.

3. Steven Ertelt, "University of Wisconsin Doctors Planned New Madison Abortion Center for Years," LifeNews.com, January 28, 2010, https://www.lifenews.com/2009/01/01/state-4764/.

4. James Thomson, Morgridge Institute for Research, https://morgridge.org/profile/james-thomson/.

5. Alliance Defending Freedom, https://web.archive.org/web/20191110090247/http://adflegal.org/detailspages/faith-and-justice-details/the-lifeguard (originally accessed as "The Lifeguard," cover story, *Faith & Justice* 4:2, July 1, 2011, http://adflegal.org/detailspages/faith-and-justice-details/the-lifeguard).

6. Ertelt, "University of Wisconsin Doctors Planned New Madison Abortion Center for Years."

7. Pat Schneider, "Plan near completion for access to abortion," *Capital Times*, February 2, 2002, p. 7, https://www.newspapers.com/image/526002534.

8. Dana Ferguson, "Abortion doctors fear successor shortage," *Milwaukee Journal Sentinel*, July 5, 2014, http://archive.jsonline.com/news/statepolitics/abortion-doctors-fear-successor-shortage-b99304541z1-265919091.html/.

9. Bruce Von Deylen, "Tensions high among pro-choice activists," *South Bend Tribune*, March 15, 1993, https://www.newspapers.com/image/520229960/.

10. Erin Banco, "MSC gives green light to new abortion clinic," *Daily Cardinal*, February 9, 2009, p. 3, https://issuu.com/the_daily_cardinal/docs/2009-02-09.

11. Joanna Salmen, "Abortion clinic opens in Madison," *Badger Herald*, January 19, 2004, https://badgerherald.com/news/2004/01/19/abortion-clinic-open/.

12. Signe Brewster, "Clinic motives under scrutiny," *Badger Herald*, February 2, 2009, https://badgerherald.com/news/2009/02/02/clinic-motives-under/.

13. Ryan J. Foley, "Doctor key to UW abortion plan leaving for Harvard," *Boston Globe*, June 14, 2010, http://archive.boston.com/news/education/higher/articles/2010/06/14/doctor_key_to_uw_abortion_plan_leaving_for_harvard/.

14. Planned Parenthood of Wisconsin v. Van Hollen, 94 F.Supp.3d 949, US District Court (W.D. Wis. 2015), https://www.leagle.com/decision/infdco20150324976.

15. Jill Stanek, "Planned Parenthood Abortionist Central to UW Late-term Abortion Scandal to Teach at Harvard," JillStanek.com, June 16, 2010, http://www.jillstanek.com/2010/06/planned-parenthood-abortionist-central-to-uw-late-term-abortion-scandal-to-teach-at-harvard/.

16. Barbara Lyons, "Abortion Program Politically, Financially Motivated," *Madison Catholic Herald*, February 26, 2009, http://www.madisoncatholicherald.org/guestcolumn/455-lyons-column.html.

17. "Univ. of Wis. Hospitals secret plan to perform second-trimester abortions unveiled," Alliance Defending Freedom, January 6, 2009, http://www.adfmedia.org/News/PRDetail/3690.

18. Judith Davidoff, "Local groups coalesce around fight to block second-trimester abortions," *Capital Times*, February 4, 2009,

https://madison.com/thecaptimes/local-groups-coalesce-around-fight-to-block-second-trimester-abortions/article_12d78a14-c2e6-5c03-afa8-3145a11239e5.html.

19. Mark Pitsch, "Ryan, Sensenbrenner urge UW Health to reconsider abortion decision," Madison.com, January 7, 2009, http://host.madison.com/news/local/govt_and_politics/blog/ryan-sensenbrenner-urge-uw-health-to-reconsider-abortion-decision/article_a7104690-0b00-5504-b1e4-d7f9827c8752.html.

20. Pro-Life Wisconsin Education Task Force, https://web.archive.org/web/20160831233733/http://www.nouwabortions.com/background.asp.

21. Staff, "Madison/UW clinic's plans for abortions questioned," *St. Paul Pioneer Press,* January 6, 2009, https://www.twincities.com/2009/01/06/madison-uw-clinics-plans-for-abortions-questioned/.

22. Lyons, "Abortion Program Politically, Financially Motivated."

23. "'Secret' University of Wisconsin plans for mid-term abortion clinic revealed," Catholic News Agency, January 7, 2009, http://www.catholicnewsagency.com/news/secret_university_of_wisconsin_plans_for_midterm_abortion_clinic_revealed/.

24. Wahlberg, "Abortion Clinic is Proposed\The UW-Meriter Facility Would Main Offer Second-Trimester Abortions."

25. Lyons, "Abortion Program Politically, Financially Motivated."

26. David Wahlberg, "Board Approves Abortion Clinic Madison Surgery Center Will Offer Second-Trimester Abortions," Madison.com, February 7, 2009, http://host.madison.com/news/board-approves-abortion-clinic-madison-surgery-center-will-offer-second/article_3c948df9-28fe-51d5-a00d-79904e422bb0.html.

27. https://web.archive.org/web/20100216002624/http:/vigilforlife-org.echristianchurches.com/documents/UWMF_public_records_late-term_abortion_Apr2009.pdf.

28. Ibid.

CHAPTER 7

1. Fr. Richard Heilman, "Origins of the Knights of Divine Mercy," RomanCatholicMan.com, November 17, 2019, http://www.romancatholicman.com/origins-of-the-knights-of-divine-mercy/.

2. Julian Quinones, Arijeta Lajka, "'What kind of society do you want to live in?': Inside the country where Down syndrome is

disappearing," CBS News, August 14, 2017, https://www.cbsnews.com/news/down-syndrome-iceland/.

CHAPTER 8

1. JillStanek.com, https://web.archive.org/web/201708270805
09/http://www.jillstanek.com/madwirtl-thumb-500x567.png.

2. JillStanek.com, https://web.archive.org/web/201303141005
15/http://www.jillstanek.com/uw%20email.jpg.

3. "UW Alums against abortion," letter to the editor, *Badger Herald*, January 30, 2009, https://badgerherald.com/opinion/2009/01/30/uw-alums-against-abo/.

4. Kelly Gunderson, "Abortion clinic faces criticism from pro-lifers," Madison.com, January 29, 2009, http://host.madison.com/daily-cardinal/news/abortion-clinic-faces-criticism-from-pro-lifers/article_94611647-8a10-5429-8baa-8e26c197c996.html.

5. "Lawmakers Decry UW Abortion Plan," *Capital Times*, January 23, 2009, http://host.madison.com/news/local/lawmakers-decry-uw-abortion-plan/article_8e6444cc-3d90-54c4-9a6c-952f9420de6c.html.

6. Alliance Defending Freedom, https://web.archive.org/web/20191110090247/http://adflegal.org/detailspages/faith-and-justice-details/the-lifeguard (originally accessed as "The Lifeguard," cover story, *Faith & Justice* 4:2, July 1, 2011, http://adflegal.org/detailspages/faith-and-justice-details/the-lifeguard).

7. Doug Erickson, "Protesters Aim to Bar Abortion Clinic," Madison.com, January 28, 2009, http://host.madison.com/news/local/protesters-aim-to-bar-abortion-clinic/article_47d50a73-02d4-5003-873b-709c6111ee97.html.

8. C. S. Lewis, *The Screwtape Letters* (first published in 1942).

9. Amy Kemery, "Activists defend Madison Clinic," *Socialist Worker*, February 8, 2009, https://socialistworker.org/2009/02/09/activists-defend-madison-clinic.

10. Pat Schneider, "Protesters Rally on Abortion Issue Activists March From UW to Proposed Clinic," *Capital Times*, February 1, 2009, http://host.madison.com/news/local/protesters-rally-on-abortion-issue-activists-march-form-uw-to/article_8ba6a7c7-3ba2-58a0-8abe-82a44655194f.html.

11. Ibid.

CHAPTER 10

1. Pat Schneider, "Protesters Rally on Abortion Issue Activists March From UW to Proposed Clinic," *Capital Times*, February 1, 2009, http://host.madison.com/news/local/protesters-rally-on-abortion-issue-activists-march-form-uw-to/article_8ba6a7c7-3ba2-58a0-8abe-82a44655194f.html.

2. "Board of Directors," *State Journal*, Madison.com, December 5, 2009, https://madison.com/board-of-directors/article_843a1cf0-e1d1-11de-b5d2-001cc4c03286.html.

3. Ryan J. Foley, "Abortion Activists Reviewed by Feds before 2009 Rally," *Wisconsin State Journal*, February 9, 2010, http://host.madison.com/wsj/news/local/govt_and_politics/abortion-activists-reviewed-by-feds-before-rally/article_bf650ac0-2bb8-11df-93fb-001cc4c03286.html.

4. Ibid.

5. Ibid.

6. Ibid.

7. Ibid.

8. Brian Sikma, "University of Wisconsin Researchers Harvested Fetal Tissue in Abortions for Experiments," MediaTrackers.org, August 31, 2015, https://web.archive.org/web/20160830090850/http://mediatrackers.org/wisconsin/2015/08/31/university-wisconsin-researchers-harvested-fetal-tissue-abortions-experiments.

9. Jane Roe, et al., Appellants, v. Henry Wade, 410 U.S. 113 (1973), Legal Information Institute, Cornell Law School, https://www.law.cornell.edu/supremecourt/text/410/113.

10. Alliance Defending Freedom, https://web.archive.org/web/20191110090247/http://adflegal.org/detailspages/faith-and-justice-details/the-lifeguard (originally accessed as "The Lifeguard," cover story, *Faith & Justice* 4:2, July 1, 2011, http://adflegal.org/detailspages/faith-and-justice-details/the-lifeguard).

11. "UPDATE: Madison Surgery Center Will Not be a Site for Second-Trimester Abortions," NBC15.com, February 6, 2009, https://www.nbc15.com/content/news/UPDATE__Madison_Surgery_Center_Will_Not_be_a_Site_for_Second-Trimester_Abortions.html.

CHAPTER 11

1. Harper Lee, *To Kill a Mockingbird* (Harper Perennial Modern Classic, 2006; J. B. Lippincott, 1960, 1st ed.).

2. Alliance Defending Freedom, https://web.archive.org/ web/20191110090247/http://adflegal.org/detailspages/faith-and-justice-details/the-lifeguard (originally accessed as "The Lifeguard," cover story, *Faith & Justice* 4:2, July 1, 2011, http://adflegal.org/ detailspages/faith-and-justice-details/the-lifeguard).

3. Jill Stanek, "Pro-life Pressure Is Stopping Late-term Abortions at UW Madison Hospital," JillStanek.com, May 14, 2009, http://www .jillstanek.com/2009/05/pro-life-pressure-is-stopping-late-term-abortions-at-uw-madison-hospital/.

4. Ibid.

5. Jill Stanek, "UW Madison Hospital Abandons Plans to Commit Late-term Abortions," JillStanek.com, May 5, 2010, http:// www.jillstanek.com/2010/05/uw-madison-hospital-abandons-plans-to-commit-late-term-abortions/.

6. Alissa Hirscher, letter to the editor, *Wisconsin State Journal*, January 26, 2010, http://host.madison.com/wsj/news/opinion/mail bag/alissa-hirscher-won-t-seek-ob-care-where-abortions-done/ article_9f0eff56-0aac-11df-b626-001cc4c03286.html.

7. Stanek, "Pro-life Pressure Is Stopping Late-term Abortions at UW Madison Hospital."

8. Alliance Defending Freedom, "The Lifeguard."

9. Ibid.

10. Stanek, "Pro-life Pressure Is Stopping Late-term Abortions at UW Madison Hospital."

11. https://web.archive.org/web/20100216002624/http:/vigil forlife-org.echristianchurches.com/documents/UWMF_public_ records_late-term_abortion_Apr2009.pdf.

12. Ibid.

13. State statute 940.04, Abortion (2001, 2011), Wisconsin State Legislature, https://docs.legis.wisconsin.gov/statutes/statutes /940/I/04.

14. "Anti-Life Legislation Defeated," Wisconsin Right to Life, https://wisconsinrighttolife.org/anti-life-legislation/.

15. https://web.archive.org/web/20100216002624/http:/vigil forlife-org.echristianchurches.com/documents/UWMF_public_ records_late-term_abortion_Apr2009.pdf.

16. Lee, *To Kill a Mockingbird*.

17. David Zucchino, "Eisenhower had a second, secret D-day message," *Los Angeles Times*, June 5, 2014, http://www.latimes.com/nation/nationnow/la-na-eisenhower-d-day-message-story.html.

CHAPTER 12

1. Alliance Defending Freedom, https://web.archive.org/web /20191110090247/http://adflegal.org/detailspages/faith-and-justice-details/the-lifeguard (originally accessed as "The Lifeguard," cover story, *Faith & Justice* 4:2, July 1, 2011, http://adflegal.org/detailspages/faith-and-justice-details/the-lifeguard).

CHAPTER 13

1. Michael J. New, "Ten Years after Obamacare, Pro-Life Concerns Are Proven Right," *National Review*, April 1, 2020, https://www.nationalreview.com/corner/ten-years-after-obamacare-pro-life-concerns-are-proven-right/.

CHAPTER 14

1. Staff, "Close to 500 Abortion Protesters Turn Out for Library Mall Rally," *Wisconsin State Journal*, February 6, 2010, http://host.madison.com/wsj/news/local/close-to-abortion-protesters-turn-out-for-library-mall-rally/article_39ce110a-1389-11df-b0a3-001cc4c03286.html.

2. Gordon Govier, "ProLife Demonstrators Mark One Year Without Abortions in Madison Surgery Center," AllGod'sPeople.com, February 7, 2010, http://www.allgodspeople.com/madison/prolife-demonstrators-mark-one-year-without-abortions-in-madison-surgery-center.html.

3. Syte Reitz, "Doug Erickson and the Wisconsin State Journal Are Up to Their Old Tricks," SyteReitz.com, February 6, 2014, http://sytereitz.com/2014/02/doug-erickson-and-the-wisconsin-state-journal-are-up-to-their-old-tricks/.

CHAPTER 15

1. Cheryl Sherry, "A church divided," *Post-Crescent*, December 5, 2004, https://www.newspapers.com/image/290639310.

2. "Priest who says he was forced to resign sues Diocese of Green Bay," *Stevens Point Journal*, Associated Press, July 16, 2006, p. 5A, https://www.newspapers.com/image/252051661/.

3. Cheryl Sherry, "Beacon of Hope embraces spirit of Vatican II," *Post-Crescent*, October 22, 2005, https://www.newspapers.com/image/?clipping_id=24413147&fcf.

4. Sherry, "A church divided."

5. Ibid.

6. Religion Notes, *Post-Crescent*, November 26, 2005, https://www.newspapers.com/image/290762962/.

CHAPTER 16

1. Samara Kalk Derby, "Madison Surgery Center Apparently Drops Late-term Abortion Plans," *Wisconsin State Journal*, May 5, 2010, http://host.madison.com/wsj/news/local/health_med_fit/madison-surgery-center-apparently-drops-late-term-abortion-plans/article_ab79b91a-58a0-11df-a9bd-001cc4c002e0.html.

2. Ibid.

3. Jill Stanek, "Update: University of WI Health Denies AG Report It Has Abandoned Plans to Commit Late-term Abortions," JillStanek.com, May 6, 2010, http://www.jillstanek.com/2010/05/update-university-of-wi-health-denies-ag-report-it-has-abandoned-plans-to-commit-late-term-abortions/.

4. Ryan J. Foley, "Doctor key to UW abortion plan leaving for Harvard," *Boston Globe*, Associated Press, June 14, 2010, http://archive.boston.com/news/education/higher/articles/2010/06/14/doctor_key_to_uw_abortion_plan_leaving_for_harvard/.

5. Derby, "Madison Surgery Center Apparently Drops Late-term Abortion Plans."

6. Stanek, "Update: University of WI Health Denies AG Report It Has Abandoned Plans to Commit Late-term Abortions."

7. Luke 1:49.

8. "How often is abortion necessary to 'save the life of the mother'?," National Right to Life, October 19, 2012, http://www.

nrlc.org/archive/abortion/pba/HowOftenAbortionNecessarySave Mother.pdf.

9. Ibid.

10. "Doctor key to UW abortion plans is leaving for Harvard," *Capital Times*, Associated Press, June 14, 2010, http://host.madison. com/ct/news/local/health_med_fit/doctor-key-to-uw-abortion-plans-is-leaving-for-harvard/article_c9ae63e6-77c6-11df-b4e1-001cc4c002e0.html.

11. Jill Stanek, "Planned Parenthood Abortionist Central to UW Late-term Abortion Scandal to Teach at Harvard," JillStanek. com, June 16, 2010, http://www.jillstanek.com/2010/06/planned-parenthood-abortionist-central-to-uw-late-term-abortion-scandal-to-teach-at-harvard/.

12. Ibid.

13. Judith Davidoff, "Madison Surgery Center will not offer second-trimester abortions," *Capital Times*, December 14, 2010, https://madison.com/ct/news/local/health_med_fit/madison-surgery-center-will-not-offer-second-trimester-abortions/article_8a1e5d32-070c-11e0-be05-001cc4c03286.html.

14. Doug Erickson, "UW Health Gives Up Search for 2nd Trimester Abortion Site," *Wisconsin State Journal*, December 13, 2010, http://host.madison.com/wsj/news/local/health_med_fit/uw-health-gives-up-search-for-nd-trimester-abortion-site/article_b7263e78-072d-11e0-ad48-001cc4c03286.html.

15. WKOW, "ProLife/ProChoice Reacts to UW Health Clinic," December 14, 2010.

16. Ibid.

CHAPTER 17

1. Planned Parenthood 2018–2019 Annual Report, https://www.plannedparenthood.org/uploads/filer_public/2e/da/2eda3f50-82aa-4ddb-acce-c2854c4ea80b/2018-2019_annual_report.pdf.

2. Wisconsin Department of Health Services, "Reported Induced Abortions in Wisconsin 2018," February 2020, https://www.dhs.wisconsin.gov/publications/p45360-18.pdf.

3. Jessica VanEgeren, "Madison passes buffer to protect women from pro-life advocates outside abortion clinics," *Capital Times*, February 26, 2014, http://host.madison.com/news/local/writers/

jessica_vanegeren/madison-passes-buffer-to-protect-women-from
-pro-life-advocates/article_d1e490f0-9f02-11e3-bebf-001a4bcf88
7a.html.

4. Britni McDonald, "Protester buffer for abortion clinics considered," NBC15.com, January 15, 2014, https://www.nbc15.com/content/news/Protester-buffer-for-abortion-clinics-considered-240 263851.html.

5. Ibid.

6. Ibid.

7. Ibid.

8. Dean Mosiman, "Madison to Cease Enforcing Protective Buffer Zone around Health Clinics," *Wisconsin State Journal*, July 3, 2014, http://host.madison.com/wsj/news/local/govt-and-politics/madison-to-cease-enforcing-protective-buffer-zone-around-health-clinics/article_8bbf3efd-b7d7-5ec5-a432-bb98d5a669b1.html.

9. Fr. Rick Heilman, "Welcome to the Garden," Miracle of Life Rosary Garden, July 21, 2011, http://www.rosarygarden.org/2011/07/welcome-to-the-garden/.

10. Ibid.

11. *Field of Dreams*, Phil Alden Robinson, director (Universal Pictures, 1989); https://www.quotes.net/movies/field_of_dreams_3901.

CHAPTER 18

1. Brian Kolodiejchuk, ed., *Mother Teresa: Come Be My Light, the Private Writings of the Saint of Calcutta* (Doubleday, 2007).

2. Erika Glover, "Live Like Mother Teresa: Finding Your Own Calcutta," Franciscan Media, March 13, 2018, https://blog.franciscan media.org/franciscan-spirit/live-like-mother-teresa-finding-your-own -calcutta.

3. Catholic News Agency, "Our Lady of Fatima," https://www.catholicnewsagency.com/saint/our-lady-of-fatima-485.

POSTSCRIPT

1. G. K. Chesterton, *Orthodoxy* (San Francisco: Ignatius; reprinted in 1995), 55.

About the Author

Steve Karlen is the campaign
director at 40 Days for Life.
After Steve helped lead a statewide coalition that prevented
the University of Wiscon-
sin Hospital and Clinics from
opening a late-term abortion
facility near the campus of his
alma mater, Steve was asked to
serve on the 40 Days for Life

headquarters team. In this role, Steve has helped spread the
40 Days for Life mission across the United States, Canada,
and Mexico.

Steve is the editor of *Day 41* magazine and the co-host
of the *40 Days for Life Podcast*. He has spoken in all fifty
states, four Canadian provinces, and Mexico City. Steve and
his work have been featured on American Family Radio,
EWTN, the Christian Broadcasting Network, NBC, CBS,
and Fox affiliates, as well as numerous newspapers and radio
stations.

Steve lives in Madison, Wisconsin, with his wife Laura
and their five children.

Be part of the beginning of the end of abortion!

PRAY MORE!

Find your closest 40 Days for Life vigil today at
40daysforlife.com/locations

READ MORE!

Keep up with saved lives, abortion worker conversions, and the pulse of the pro-life movement by receiving *DAY 41*, the quarterly magazine, for FREE! Sign up at
40daysforlife.com/magazine

LISTEN MORE!

Download the weekly 40 Days for Life podcast for free. Guests include Peter Kreeft, Eric Metaxas, Alan Keyes, Father Paul Scalia, Benjamin Watson, Lila Rose, and many more. Listen on any podcast app, the 40 Days for Life app, or at

40daysforlife.com/podcast

Get special discounted copies of this book and the national best-seller *The Beginning of the End of Abortion* and great pro-life gear at

40daysforlifegear.com

Invite Steve Karlen or another member of the 40 Days for Life headquarters team to speak at your event by emailing
media@40daysforlife.com
Find out more at 40daysforlife.com